WICCA
CANDLE MAGIC

A BEGINNER'S GUIDE TO CANDLE SPELLCRAFT

LISA CHAMBERLAIN

STERLING ETHOS
New York

STERLING ETHOS
New York

ISBN 978-1-4549-3533-9
ISBN 978-1-4549-3534-6 (e-book)

Distributed in Canada by Sterling Publishing Co., Inc.
C/o Canadian Manda Group, 664 Annette Street
Toronto, Ontario, Canada M6S 2C8
Distributed in the United Kingdom by GMC Distribution Services
Castle Place, 166 High Street, Lewes, East Sussex, England BN7 1XU
Distributed in Australia by NewSouth Books
University of New South Wales, Sydney, NSW 2052, Australia

For information about custom editions, special sales and premium
and corporate purchases, please contact Sterling Special Sales
at 800-805-5489 or specialsales@sterlingpublishing.com.

Manufactured in Canada

10 9 8 7 6 5 4 3 2 1

sterlingpublishing.com

Design by Christine Heun and Sharon Leigh Jacobs
Picture credits—see page 123

For all who dare to let their light shine

CONTENTS

M. Bowley.

INTRODUCTION

FOR WITCHES AND MANY NON-WITCHES ALIKE, THERE'S JUST something about a candle flame that inspires a sense of mystery. This guide will help you tap into the source of that mystery and harness the power of candles to increase your well-being.

Whether you realize it or not, you most likely started practicing a very popular form of candle magic in childhood—the blowing out of candles on a birthday cake. While this simple tradition isn't exactly like working a spell, it demonstrates the basic gist of magic: communicating a desire to the Universe in a focused, ritualized manner.

Magic is a way of harnessing the unseen energy of the Universe to effect a change in the physical world, whether that change is tangible, such as more money in your pocket, or intangible, such as a more positive outlook on a situation that seems to be keeping you down. Candle magic uses the power of the Element of Fire to send an intention into the Universe, and it is a particularly beginner-friendly form of spellwork.

Wiccans and other Witches have long known that candles are great tools for transformative magic. Candles are excellent symbols of the cocreative relationship of the Elements. The solid base of the candle represents Earth, as does the wick, which provides the grounding mechanism for the flame to stay alive. As the wax melts, it emulates the shape-shifting qualities of the Element of Water, which can be found in solid, liquid, or gaseous form. The smoke released from the burning wick evokes the Element of Air, one of the ingredients needed for the flame to exist in the first place. And the flame itself, of course, represents Fire.

Although this guide is written from a Wiccan perspective, it's important to note that not all Wiccans consider themselves to be magical practitioners, Wiccans, or Witches. Some only use candles for ritual and devotional purposes. Others may practice magic independently from any religious or ritualized context. No matter how you describe your spiritual practice, however, this guide is for you if you're interested in learning more about the magical qualities of fire and its uses in candle magic.

Since candle magic is first and foremost a form of fire magic, we will start this beginner's guide with an introduction to the energy and magical properties of the Fire. In part one, we'll take a brief look at fire's role in the magical lives of our ancient pagan ancestors as well as other occult traditions that have inspired the modern practice of candle magic. We'll also cover basic principles of magic, including the role of color in candle spells.

Part two offers a guide to choosing candles and preparing them for spellwork as well as tips for making the most out of your candle magic experience. In part three, you'll find a selection of candle spells to try on your own and ideas for DIY candle-related crafts. Hopefully, these pages will leave you inspired and excited to begin using candle magic to transform your reality!

Blessed Be.

PART ONE

SACRED FLAMES

THE WONDER OF FIRE

OUR EARLIEST HUMAN ANCESTORS LIVED FOR HUNDREDS OF thousands of years before discovering how to create fire and harness its power. Before that, fire was only witnessed as a force of Nature, roaring across a vast savannah or climbing the heights of an ancient forest. All it took was a single bolt of lightning to create a potential catastrophe for people and animals alike. Imagine how astounding it must have been to discover how to control such a force—not to mention the sudden possibilities for more favorable living conditions! Cooked food, warmer shelters, and protection from predators were just the first of many benefits that fire would come to provide. And though in the twenty-first century we tend to take these things for granted, there is still something mystical—even magical—about fire, even for many people who aren't aware that magic is real.

Although archaeologists believe the use of fire may go back a million years or more, no one knows exactly when or how humans first learned to create and control fire. This mystery is at the heart of many origin myths from around the world. In these tales, humans don't get the credit for this momentous achievement. Fire is often acquired from elsewhere. Often, deities or other mythological figures "give" fire to humans. One well-known example is the ancient Greek story of Prometheus, who steals fire from the lightning of Zeus and gives it to humankind to advance civilization. Spider Grandmother, an important figure in many Native American cultures, steals fire from the Sun in a Cherokee myth and gives it to the people so that they may be able to see in the dark. A Hindu story tells of the immortal figure Mātariśvan (or Agni) who brings the fire from its hidden place in the sky to the Earth and teaches the people how to kindle it using sticks.

A recurring motif in these ancient stories is that the fire is stolen, rather than willingly granted. The culprits are often mythological animals, such as Nanabozho from Ojibwe legends, a spirit who takes the form of a hare or rabbit and tricks a neighboring community into sharing their fire with him, and the (praying) Mantis of the San people of southern Africa, who steals fire from under the wing of its guardian, the Ostrich. A tale from the Wurundjeri people of Australia describes how the Crow steals live coals from the Karatgurk—seven mythological sisters who represent the Pleiades constellation.

In so many of these myths, there seems to be something about the power and mystery inherent to fire that requires quick, clever thinking to gain the use of it. Knowledge of how to create and control fire for oneself wasn't made available to just anyone, and more often than not, the characters who have the fire (whether gods, animals, or other people) are quite unwilling to share it. Was this due to an awareness of fire's dangers and the accidental or intentional harm it could cause? Or was it perhaps a universal perception of fire as a coveted supernatural phenomenon that needs to be guarded, in a similar manner to a sorcerer's stone or the Holy

Grail? Whatever the case, it's clear that the immense power of fire was not lost on the cultures that gave birth to these stories.

Our primal connection to fire has largely faded from our awareness since those early days of our existence. Yet despite all the modern technology we use to heat our homes, illuminate our living spaces, and power our electronic devices, we still enjoy the ambience of fire in the form of indoor hearths, outdoor bonfires, and, of course, candles of all kinds. Gazing into a fire, whether it be a still, single flame or a crackling campfire, can be calming and meditative—a way to transcend ordinary reality and connect with the Universal energies that make the phenomenon of fire possible.

Perhaps this is part of why fire remains an important ceremonial component in many religions around the world, both ancient and modern. The practice of keeping an eternal flame (usually a torch or other small fire) has been part of religious traditions since the days of ancient Persia. Eternal flames were present in ancient Roman, Chinese, and indigenous Mexican traditions, and are found today in the form of sanctuary lamps in Jewish synagogues and tabernacle candles in Catholic churches.

Fire is also a traditional part of funeral rites in some cultures. In Hinduism, the body of the deceased is burned to encourage the soul to move on to its next incarnation. The fire in cremation rituals provides a definitive ending to the physical existence of the departed, purifying the spirit and preparing for rebirth. We can see something of this symbolism in the mythical phoenix—a bird that bursts into flames, is entirely incinerated, and is then reborn out of the ashes of its previous incarnation.

Candles, of course, are used widely in religious practices. There are always candles lit at Catholic masses, with particular emphasis during Advent and Lent, and worshippers light votive candles to honor the Virgin Mary and many saints. Candles are part of Jewish Shabbat rituals and are the focal point of

Hanukkah, where a candelabra called the menorah is used to mark each of the holiday's eight nights. During the Hindu festival of Diwali, candles and small oil lamps known as *diyas* are lit to celebrate the return of light over darkness. In the modern African American holiday of Kwanzaa, seven candles represent the seven principles of pan-African culture. All around the world, candles are kept lit at religious altars and shrines of all kinds—from grand, ornate temples to a simple corner shelf in a humble home.

Fire often takes center stage in Wiccan ritual as well, whether it's in the form of a Sabbat bonfire outdoors, a small fire within a cauldron, a sacred candle marked with tea lights, or several candles on the altar to honor deities and Elements. And, of course, candles are often the focal points in magic spells. There are elaborate spells, using many candles along with several other ingredients, and much less involved spells that may require only one simple white tea light. The spells in this guide have one or more candles as their central focus, although some will involve other easy-to-find items like essential oils and dried herbs. All are suitable for beginners and more advanced practitioners alike and can be tailored to fit your individual magical style.

Before we dive into the spellwork, however, we'll take some time to explore the magical relationship to fire that our ancestors experienced, highlighting traditions and beliefs that paved the way for the use of fire in modern Wiccan ritual and magical practices. We'll also outline some helpful magical concepts, including the Hermetic Principles and the role of color in magic, and apply these ideas to candle spellwork for a clearer sense of how candle magic works.

ANCIENT AND MODERN FIRE WORSHIP

EVEN FOR MANY NON-MAGICAL PEOPLE, FIRE HAS AN undeniably enigmatic quality. Fire is an event, rather than a physical substance, even though it can come into contact with physical things (and needs them to continue burning). Fire is the visible effect of an invisible process: combustion, which results from the right combination of heat, oxygen, and fuel. In this process, the fuel, which can be anything capable of burning, is transformed from a solid state into a gaseous state, releasing heat and light as it transforms. Fire is a force of Nature. Fire is not biologically "alive" in the technical sense of the word, but those who are attuned to the energy of its presence commonly regard it as a living entity or spirit.

Fire is one of the classical elements recognized by the ancient Greeks and plays a similarly central role in Chinese, Hindu, and Buddhist belief systems, among others. It has interesting paradoxical relationships with its fellow elements. Fire can consume Earth in the form of plant matter, such as trees or fossils, but Earth in the form of soil can also put it out. It is often extinguished by water, yet water is also released in the form of vapor when something burns. Fire is fed by air in the form of oxygen and can grow quickly with a strong wind, yet depending on the amount of heat and fuel, Air can also snuff it out.

Fire is also the only element that doesn't exist on its own—it must be created by the combination of Earth (fuel) and Air (oxygen) to remain active. It's also the only element that is constantly in motion, continually transforming one thing into something else. Fire is tangible yet can't be touched without bodily harm. It's arguably the most dangerous of the elements for its potential to cause immediate and irreparable damage.

Perhaps fire's biggest paradox is its ability to both destroy and create. In fact, this is ultimately its role in Nature, as seen in the cycles of forest and grassland fires. These fires certainly devastate, but in doing so, they purify ecosystems of invasive species and tree-killing insects and diseases, and they replenish the soil with nutrients. They clear more room for new plant and animal life to thrive. Before human intervention created massive imbalances, the fire cycles in the wild occurred regularly and were necessary for sustaining life in those areas.

These mysterious properties of fire were surely reflected upon by our ancient pagan ancestors, whose beliefs and cultural traditions significantly influenced modern Wiccan practices. We

can see from recorded traditions, some of which still survive today in one form or another, that fire was very much revered as a sacred presence in the spiritual lives of pre-Christian peoples. It is worth taking a closer look at some of these beliefs and practices, as it is this ancient understanding of fire that forms the spiritual roots of candle magic.

ANCIENT PAGAN
FIRE TRADITIONS

ROUND THE GLOBE, PARTICULARLY IN THE AREAS OF EUROPE whose cultures came to inspire Wicca and other modern Pagan religions, fire was significant to many aspects of spiritual and magical life. Deity worship, divination, magic within the home, and communal ritual celebrations all involved fire. Some of these beliefs and traditions can still be seen in one form or another in modern Pagan practice today.

Fire Divination

Fire divination, or pyromancy, was practiced in many different forms throughout the ancient pagan world. The movement and appearance of flames and smoke from a fire could be read for information about current and future events. These omens might appear as shapes within the flames of a ritual fire or revealed in the behavior of the smoke. Generally, smoke that rose in a straight, single plume from a fire was considered a good sign, while thick, swirling smoke would be interpreted as a warning. Divination via smoke, also known as capnomancy, is still in practice in parts of New England, where some follow the tradition of predicting the weather based on the behavior of chimney smoke.

Many forms of pyromancy involved animals and plants. Many religious rituals included animal sacrifices, and fire divination was often performed as part of the process. In ancient Greece, priests read the smoke produced by the fire used to burn the sacrificial animal for signs. In parts of China as well as in the Celtic world, specific bones of certain animals were burned so that the seers could read the cracks resulting from the fire. The Celts also burned oak and mistletoe branches, using the smoke to prophesy the future, while the Babylonians used cedar branches. The ancient Greeks and Romans divined messages from the noise of a fire made with bay laurel leaves. The quieter the fire, the less positive the outcome of the situation in question was considered to be.

Even salt was sometimes used for pyromancy. A Scottish tradition holds that on Imbolc night, the celebration of winter's end, each member of the family would cast some salt into the fire. The main purpose of the ritual was to protect the home for the coming year, but signs of the future could be read in the way the fire responded to the salt, with a specific message for each member of the family who participated. Another hearth fire tradition held that cinders flying out of the fire could be read as omens based on their shapes.

The Sacred Hearth Fire

The hearth, where such divination rituals were performed, was itself a central focus of fire magic, just as it was the center of day-to-day life within the home. Serving as both heat source and cookstove, the fire within the hearth was vital to the family's survival and was kept banked overnight with ashes so that it could be stoked back to life in the morning. Before the invention of matches and lighters, starting a fire was usually a labor-intensive process, so the availability of fire was never taken for granted. It was considered bad luck to let the fire go out completely, except for a ritual. Rituals that involved intentionally extinguishing an "old" fire and lighting a fire for the new year usually happened once a year.

The sacred energy of the fire in the hearth made it an important center for many types of magic. The hearth was considered an energetic entry point to the home, and objects of significance were magically charmed to protect the home and its inhabitants from harmful spirits, black magic, house fires, and other disasters. Items found hidden in the chimney breasts of old houses in Europe, North America, and Australia have included shoes, clothing, "witch bottles," and written charms. Sigil magic, in the form of circles and other protective symbols inscribed on the hearth, was also used to keep evil spirits from entering through the chimney. It is believed that some of these practices continued in the United Kingdom into the early twentieth century.

In many traditions, the spirits of ancestors and other benevolent nonphysical beings served as guardians of the hearth and the home. Candles would be lit at the hearth to honor these spirits, and they were thanked for their service with offerings of milk or mead. A hearth guardian might be represented by a small statue placed near the hearth, with offerings placed in a bowl beside it.

Fire Deities

Ancient cultures recognized and honored different types of fire, which were often represented by different deities. The fire of the hearth, for example, was typically the realm of the divine feminine, presided over by the goddess Hestia among the Greeks and the goddess Vesta among the Romans. Like many hearth deities, Vesta was also the goddess of the home and family, a logical association as the hearth was literally the center of the home as well as the gathering place for the family. Vesta's importance is underlined by the temple built in her honor, where women known as the Vestal Virgins tended to the "sacred fire of Vesta" around the clock. This fire represented the longevity and well-being of Rome under Vesta's protection, and punishments for letting it die out were severe.

Hearth goddesses are found in cultures around the world and include Cerridwen, the shape-shifting Welsh goddess of the cauldron; Saulė, who was a Sun goddess in Slavic folklore; and the Japanese fire goddess Fuchi, another figure central to the home and family. Fuchi is said to live permanently in the hearth, and for that reason the fire must never be allowed to go out completely. Many kitchen goddesses, such as Fornax, the Roman goddess of ovens, are also honored as hearth goddesses in modern Pagan practices.

Another essential type of fire was that of the forge. It is perhaps the ultimate representation of the creative and transformative powers of fire. At a forge, metals were heated to be shaped into tools, weapons, jewelry, and other items. The fire of the forge was typically the domain of the divine masculine and of gods such as Lugh, a patron Celtic god of blacksmiths and artisans, and Goibniu, the divine Celtic blacksmith who made weapons and arms for the warriors.

The Greek Hephaestus, god of sculptors and metalworkers, was a blacksmith who was said to have built his forge under a volcano. His Roman counterpart, Vulcan, also kept his forge in a similar location, and his name is at the root of the English word *volcano*. In addition to the fire of the forge, Vulcan was directly associated with fire's dangerous aspects. Romans appealed to him to keep their households and all of Rome safe from any threat of fire.

Not all cultures drew such gender distinctions when it came to fire deities. The Celtic goddess Brighid is guardian of the hearth and home as well as the goddess of "smithcraft," or metalworking. Very much a fire goddess, she was born with a tower of flame reaching from her head to heaven and is known in some Celtic Pagan traditions as the "keeper of the sacred flame." Furthermore, there are plenty of goddesses associated with volcanos, including the Greco-Roman Aetna, the Japanese hearth goddess Fuchi, mentioned earlier, and the Hawaiian Pele. Through the fire of her volcanoes, Pele is both a destroyer and a builder, devouring old land and creating new land in the process.

Festivals of Fire

Fire was an integral part of many pagan festivals that marked important turning points in seasonal and agricultural cycles. For those living in northern climates, fire was both a literal and symbolic source of light and heat throughout long winters. The Yule celebrations of the ancient Germanic cultures, which welcomed the end of the darkest days of the year, made the hearth fire a central focus. A special log, usually made of oak, was decorated with evergreen branches and consecrated with ale or cider before being placed on the hearth. The burning of the Yule log could last up to twelve days and was believed to bring good luck in the coming year.

Bonfires were at the center of many celebrations as well, particularly in Germanic and Celtic communities. The Norse honored the summer solstice, the longest day of the year, with torchlight processions to a bonfire, where the festivities continued until the following dawn. In many Germanic areas, these festivities included a "sun wheel," which was constructed from a ball of straw or a wagon wheel, lit on fire, and rolled downhill into a body of water.

Perhaps the most well-known bonfire traditions took place in Celtic areas at the feast of Beltane. During this feast, cattle were driven along a path between two giant fires to purify and protect them from accidents and disease. Druids tended the fires, speaking magical incantations to ensure the cattle's well-being for the coming summer. This process was repeated at Samhain as the cattle were returned to their winter pastures. People would jump over fires to ensure fertility and good luck for themselves as well. Beltane was also the time for households to extinguish and then renew their hearth fires, traditionally from a central bonfire. Members of the community lit torches using this bonfire, carried them back to the communities, and shared them with each household. In this manner, everyone's hearth fire was created from the same source.

Candles, once they were widely available, also became part of many pagan holiday traditions. At Imbolc, candles were lit at the hearth and in each window of the house at sundown and kept burning until sunrise. At Samhain, candles left in windows welcomed the spirits of ancestors who were said to wander the night and look in on their families, whereas candles placed in hollowed-out root vegetables frightened off unwanted spirits.

FIRE IN WICCAN
BELIEF AND PRACTICE

THE BELIEFS AND PRACTICES COLLECTIVELY KNOWN AS
Wicca come from various influences and are always evolving
with each new generation. As noted already, many traditions from
our pagan past have seen a reemergence through the birth and
evolution of Wicca and other modern Pagan religions. The Wiccan
Wheel of the Year and the association of the divine masculine with
the Sun and Fire are rooted in these pre-Christian belief systems.

Other major influences on Wicca, particularly when it comes
to magic, come through ancient esoteric systems as well as new
spiritual discoveries made by occult scholars and mystics, whose
work has been studied and expanded over the centuries. This body
of wisdom is often referred to as the Western Mystery Tradition
and includes elements from Kabbalah, Gnosticism, Hermeticism,
and other spiritual philosophies. The Wiccan concept of Fire as an
Elemental energy originates here, along with several ideas relating
to magic that we will discuss shortly.

There are many widely varying traditions within contemporary Wiccan practice. With the exception of some covens (particularly those following a Traditional Wiccan path like Gardnerian
or Alexandrian Wicca), it's accurate to say that no two practices
are exactly alike. Nonetheless, the following beliefs and practices
related to the power of Fire are fairly standard among covens and
solitary Wiccans, whether they follow Traditional or eclectic paths.

Note: If you live in the southern hemisphere, use this list to learn the dates for the Sabbats in your area.

YULE: June 20–22
IMBOLC: August 1–2
OSTARA: September 21–23
BELTANE: October 31–November 1
LITHA: December 20–23
LAMMAS: February 1–2
MABON: March 19–21
SAMHAIN: April 30–May 1

The Sun God and the Sabbats

Many solar deities are associated with fire, including the Wiccan God in his Sun God aspect. The Sun God is the provider of light and heat, which plant and animal life need to grow and thrive. The eight Sabbats of the Wiccan Wheel of the Year, which mark the turning points of the solar cycle, honor the Sun's journey: from its lowest point at Yule, when much of life on Earth is still and dormant, to its highest point at Litha, when all is thriving, and back around again to the Sun's seeming disappearance from the land. The seasonal changes that result from this journey are mythologized as manifestations of the Sun God's birth, life, death, and rebirth. (Each Sabbat also honors the role of the Goddess in these solar cycles in her Mother Earth aspect, but the divine feminine takes her own center stage as the Triple Goddess at the lunar Esbat celebrations.)

The solar cycle is the focus of four of these Sabbats—the solstices (Yule and Litha) and the equinoxes (Ostara and Mabon). The other four Sabbats (Imbolc, Beltane, Lammas, and Samhain) occur on the cross-quarter days between these solar points. In some traditions, these are referred to as the "Earth festivals," yet they are borrowed largely from the ancient Celtic fire festivals described above. In more ways than one, the energy of Fire is at the core of the Wheel of the Year. The ritual fires we light on the Sabbats remind us of the transformational energies underlying the eternal cycle of life, death, and rebirth.

Elemental Fire

As discussed earlier, Fire is one of the classical Elements, which ancient philosophers described as being the core substances that make up everything on Earth. (The term *classical* typically refers to the ancient Greek model of elements, but again, the general idea is found in many belief systems.) The development of alchemy, an esoteric philosophical tradition that eventually gave rise to chemistry, was rooted in this framework, as were other occult disciplines throughout history. These disciplines include ceremonial magic, which inspired the invocation of Earth, Air, Fire, Water, and Spirit in Wiccan ritual.

The word *Element* and the names of the classical Elements themselves are often capitalized in Wiccan writing to distinguish them from their everyday contexts (such as "a glass of water" or "the humid air"). The Elements are viewed primarily as distinct and powerful living energies and can be perceived by those who are attuned to them. While any physical amount of water, air, earth, or fire contains the energetic quality of the Element, this energy has to be spiritually activated before being used in ritual and magic.

The integration of the Elements into Wiccan magic is rooted more in the Western Mystery Tradition than in ancient pagan traditions. Yet animism—the perception that natural objects such as lakes, rivers, trees, and stones have spirits—was prevalent throughout the pre-Christian world, as were beliefs in magical beings such as gnomes, sprites, fairies, and nymphs. Centuries ago, occult scholars began to associate these beings with the classical elements and categorized them according to where they lived. Air spirits were called sylphs, Water spirits were undines, and Earth spirits were all classified as gnomes. Fire spirits were given the name *salamanders*, which are said to resemble (but are not the same as) the salamanders we're familiar with in the mundane world. Those who visually perceive salamanders say they are lizard-shaped and appear to have tongues of flame, although some see these entities as tiny balls of light.

These beings are referred to variously as "Elementals," "Elemental spirits," or "Elemental beings," and some Witches and other modern Pagans may call upon them in ritual or magical work. However, connecting energetically with these beings was traditionally a potentially risky venture, as they could be mischievous and might have their own agendas independent of a magician's desires. In contemporary Wicca, it's more common to invoke and interact with the pure, sacred energy of the Elements themselves, rather than with their associated entities.

Of these energies, Fire is perhaps the easiest for beginning Witches to sense and arguably the most delightful to work magic with.

Candles in Wiccan Ritual

Fire is always present in one form or another during Sabbats, Esbats, and other ritual occasions. Outdoor rituals, particularly coven or other group rituals, typically feature a bonfire in the center of the sacred circle. For most solitary practitioners, however, candles serve to bring the energy of Fire.

Candles may also mark the ritual circle, whether indoors or outdoors, if space permits. This may be done with just four sturdy jar or pillar candles marking the cardinal points of the circle, or the circle's entire boundary can be marked with tea lights. (Note: Marking the circle can enhance the atmosphere of ritual very powerfully, but it does require extra caution and is not recommended for situations where small children or pets might come scampering by.) The Element of Fire is often invoked with a candle while casting the sacred circle, though in some traditions, the wand or athame, a ritual knife with a double-edged blade, may be used.

Candles also frequently represent the Goddess and the God on the altar. Gold and red commonly represent the God, while white and silver are for the Goddess, though some Wiccans use yellow and green, respectively, or choose other colors depending on their personal associations with the deities. In traditions where the Goddess is considered the central deity, she is often represented with three candles—white for her Maiden aspect, red for the Mother, and black for the Crone. Witches may also designate a candle for one or more specific deities they have a personal affinity or relationship with, such as a purple or white candle dedicated to the Greek goddess Athena or a dark green candle for the Celtic god Cernunnos.

Candles may be used to represent the four cardinal directions as well, with green or brown most commonly representing North, yellow for East, red for South, and blue for West. Alternatively, these candles may be associated with the four Elements, each of which is associated with one of the four directions. In both uses, Fire itself is typically represented with a red, orange, or gold candle on the altar. Some Wiccans will also dedicate a candle to the "Fifth Element" of Spirit, often called Akasha, either in addition to or in place of the Goddess and God candles. The Spirit candle may be black, white, silver, or purple.

Plenty of candles may be used outside of the circle to add more light and ambience to the proceedings. This is true for spellwork as well, which is where we will now turn our focus for the remainder of this guide.

WICCAN FIRE MAGIC

FIRE IS A MASCULINE, PROJECTIVE ENERGY AND IS ASSOCI-
ated with love, passion, sexuality, drive, courage, enthusiasm,
willpower, health, strength, physical energy, and creativity. Candle
spells are often focused on these areas of life, but fire magic is also
used in workings for protection, success, and personal growth.

As an Elemental energy and as a physical phenomenon, Fire
works magic through its functions of illumination, elimination,
and transformation. Fire sheds light and can literally and meta-
phorically illuminate what was previously unseen. This is evident
in the many traditions of divination around the world involving
fire. This function also makes it an excellent energy to work with
in spells for clarity, whether about a specific situation or about
aspects of one's self that have been operating at the subconscious

level. This kind of magical work is called shadow work, and it examines the hidden patterns influencing the way we respond to life's events. With the insight gained from shadow work, we can make different choices and therefore transform our reality.

In its function of elimination, Fire seems to cause all but the most dense and solid matter to vanish, leaving nothing but charred remains and ashes in its wake. In actuality, we know that the matter being burned is simply being transformed into a different state, ultimately disappearing from our awareness and our experience of reality. This eliminative function makes Fire ideal for use in banishing work, whether you want to be rid of an annoying energetic attachment, a bad habit, or leftover feelings from a relationship that has ended.

Candle spells are particularly potent for this kind of magical goal. Many candle spells involve burning paper, which might have words or symbols representing what you wish to banish. The energy of the flame symbolically consumes what you want to eliminate. On a magical level, this elimination also clears your field of reality for new manifestations to occur, much as a forest fire clears the way for new growth. A related type of fire magic is the burning of herbs or specific woods to purify a physical space or a person's energy field. In this case, the smoke from the fire is what clears away the unwanted energy.

Fire transforms one state of matter into another. As the wax of a candle is consumed in the flame, it turns from solid to liquid to gas. Metals heated in a forge are given new shapes, changing from raw ore into tools, jewelry, and works of art. Likewise, we can transform our circumstances through the magical application of Fire energy, taking the raw material of our desire and shaping it into manifested form.

Finally, the properties inherent to Fire can be used to repel or attract. Protection spells may rely on the innate danger of Fire to keep unwanted people or energy at bay. Spells to draw new energy and positive influences into one's life work with the attractive nature of Fire. On a physical level, this is easily demonstrated in the fluttering of moths toward a candle flame, but it's also apparent in the functioning of the candle itself: the heat from the flame draws the wax from the base ever upward through the wick. Herbs or flowers as well as wishes written on paper can be burned for the purposes of attraction. In this type of magic, the combustion of the ingredients sends their specific magical energies, along with your intention, out into the Universe to attract the outcome you desire.

MAGICAL WISDOM
TRADITIONS

CANDLE MAGIC, LIKE ANY OTHER FORM OF MAGIC, WORKS because of various aspects of physical and nonphysical reality. One very useful framework for understanding these aspects comes from the esoteric discipline of Hermeticism, a set of ideas attributed to an ancient Egyptian figure called Hermes Trismegistus. These ideas have informed the Western Mystery Tradition over the centuries. Beginners to magic today can particularly benefit from studying a book called the *Kybalion*, a more recent, condensed take on the core concepts found in Hermeticism. Published in the early twentieth century, the *Kybalion* lays out the seven Hermetic Principles (also known as the Hermetic Laws), which describe how the Universe works at the most basic level of reality.

The principle that Witches are probably most familiar with, whether they realize it or not, is the Principle of Correspondence. It is summed up in the well-known phrase "as above, so below" (though the full phrase is actually "as above, so below; as below, so above"). This line describes the relationship between visible and invisible reality. According to Hermeticism, the Universe contains several planes of reality, which are broadly categorized as the physical, mental, and spiritual planes. These planes do not exist separately from each other, but rather influence each other; what exists on one plane must exist in one form or another on the other planes as well. Therefore, what is found "above" on the mental or spiritual planes will also be found "below" on the physical plane.

A related idea is that of the relationship between microcosm and macrocosm, in which everything in existence is considered to be a miniature version of the entire Universe. This idea is encapsulated in another Hermetic phrase: "While All is in THE ALL, it is equally true that THE ALL is in All." If you visualize your intended goal with clarity and focus, you create its existence on the mental plane. If you then use a candle spell to send that intention forth onto the Universe actively, it now also exists on the spiritual plane. This change on the spiritual plane then works its way through the linear time and physical space of the material plane until it is manifested.

Another crucial concept for the beginning magician is the Principle of Mentalism, which states that "the ALL is Mind; the Universe is Mental." In other words, everything in the Universe is ultimately made up of consciousness. This consciousness, which is another way of saying "energy," is the conduit through which our intentions travel from the physical point of spellwork to the spiritual plane. As conscious beings who have the capacity for independent thought, we have the powerful potential to create our desired reality when we join our clear, focused intentions with the energy of Universal consciousness.

Candles make for excellent messengers of our magical intentions. As the wax of the candle base melts, the conscious energy of the intention is pulled upward through the wick and then intensified by the heat of the flame as it is released into the nonphysical world. If you really attune yourself to your spellwork, you can usually feel a distinct energy around the altar space throughout the candle's burn time and even afterwards. This energy is a signal that the consciousness of the intention is merging with the Universal mind. This is the first step toward manifestation on the physical plane.

The Principle of Vibration is also key to the workings of magic, and candle magic in particular. This is the understanding that everything in the Universe is constantly in motion in the form of vibration, an ancient concept that modern scientific discoveries have confirmed. Another way to say it is that all of reality is composed of energy (or consciousness) that vibrates at a particular rate—even objects that appear to be perfectly still. The *Kybalion* states that "nothing rests; everything moves; everything vibrates." When it comes to most solid objects, this vibrational movement is too slow for human senses to perceive, but it's easy to sense the vibrations of a candle flame, even when it's perfectly still.

Vibration is important to magic for several reasons. Perhaps most significantly, the "everything" referred to in "everything vibrates" includes *thoughts*. Thoughts vibrate at specific frequencies, and it's easy to tell whether their frequencies are high or low by the way thinking them makes you feel. Your thoughts during spellwork are the most essential aspect of the work and should always be focused on enjoying your desired outcome, rather than questions about whether the outcome is truly possible. If you're filled with doubtful or self-defeating thoughts, the vibrational frequency of those thoughts will accompany your magical intention, which will then translate as doubt, rather than belief, in the Universal mind. Spellwork under these circumstances is rarely, if ever, successful.

THE ROLE OF COLOR

THE PRINCIPLE OF VIBRATION IS ALSO KEY TO CANDLE MAGIC due to the role of color in candle spells. For centuries, certain colors have been associated with certain intangible qualities or events, such as love, luck, wealth, and death. Red has commonly been associated with love and passion. It is the color of blood and therefore of the heart. Pink, which is a combination of red and white, is a softer color, and has associations with friendship and the lighter feelings of romance. And while green is a slang term for money in the United States due to the color of its paper currency, the color itself has long been associated with abundance in many parts of the world because of the predominantly green colors of the Earth during the growing season.

Wiccan systems assign magical properties and other associations to every color of the traditional rainbow or color spectrum as well as many shades in between primary and secondary colors. Lavender, for example, is an offshoot of violet that can assist with challenges involving education, particularly in writing. Brown is associated with endurance and strength, and—as another Earth color—with abundance as well. The logic behind these correspondences can vary, and not all Witches use the same correspondences, but the Principle of Vibration is ultimately at the root of these links between color, property, and magical purpose.

Colors are bands of light vibrating at different frequencies, which the human eye can observe. Each frequency has particular characteristics suitable for specific purposes. The frequencies of red and

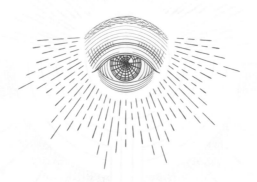

pink, for example, have been shown to resonate with the vibrations of loving feelings in the physical body, while the cheering effect of yellow's frequency can be used to raise one's spirits.

Another interesting fact about color is that it only becomes "color" when seen by the eye. It's the anatomy of the eye and its coordination with the brain that turns the band of light into what we perceive as a particular color. In this sense, when used in magic, the color serves as a connection between the self (or the "microcosm," the individual point of consciousness) and the larger Universe (or the "macrocosm," the Universal mind). And because color can also affect brain waves, cause physical changes in the body, and impact mood and behavior, it is an especially powerful force in the Universe to harness for magical purposes.

Combining the vibration of your intention with the vibrational frequency of a specific color can produce changes in the material world, whether in the form of money coming in, an injury or illness healing, or relationships improving. For example, say you're having trouble with a roommate, and neither of you is able to move elsewhere for the foreseeable future. You could work a spell to help the two of you get along better. You might choose a blue candle, since blue is magically associated with peace and harmony in the home as well as communication. Blue, when used in color therapy, has been shown to be soothing to the body, lowering the heart rate and regulating high body temperatures. Blue is also the color of the Element of Water, which is typically a soothing presence, particularly in the form of natural bodies of water like a shimmering blue ocean.

Between the physiological effects of looking at this color and the message that blue sends to the spiritual realm, you have a potent tool for bringing about the change you seek in your roommate relationship. As for what will happen as a result of the spell, the manifestation could take many forms. Perhaps in a day or two, your roommate seeks you out for a heart-to-heart talk about the source of your disagreement. Or perhaps it's you who finally feels calm and peaceful enough to initiate the reconciliation. Alternatively, your roommate may suddenly announce that they will be moving out after all. The results of magical work can seem rather mundane or ordinary, or they may seem to come very unexpectedly— from "out of the blue." If nothing at all happens for a long time, you may need to examine whether you are unnecessarily holding onto a grudge or whether you had doubts about the spell while you were working it. Remember, thoughts are also active vibrations, and they impact the degree to which your magic succeeds.

The following table outlines some tried-and-true associations between colors and their magical properties. Beginning Wiccans often find that working with widely known and widely shared associations strengthens the power of their intention setting during ritual. After a while, you'll start to have an intuitive appreciation for the characteristics and "vibe" of each color, and eventually you'll be able to choose the most appropriate color for your work without having to consult any resources. That being said, if you have personal associations with colors that differ from those provided here, then go with what makes the most intuitive sense for you.

WICCAN COLOR MAGIC
TABLE OF CORRESPONDENCES

COLOR	QUALITIES	USES IN MAGIC
RED	Passion, courage, strength, intense emotions	Love, physical energy, health, willpower
ORANGE	Energy, attraction, vitality, stimulation	Adaptability to sudden changes, encouragement, power
YELLOW	Intellect, inspiration, imagination, knowledge	Communication, confidence, divination, study
GREEN	Abundance, growth, wealth, renewal, balance	Prosperity, employment, fertility, health, good luck
BLUE	Peace, truth, wisdom, protection, patience	Healing, psychic ability, harmony in the home, understanding
VIOLET	Spirituality, wisdom, devotion, peace, idealism	Divination, enhancing nurturing qualities, balancing sensitivity
WHITE	Peace, innocence, illumination, purity	Cleansing, clarity, establishing order, spiritual growth and understanding

COLOR	QUALITIES	USES IN MAGIC
BLACK	Dignity, force, stability, protection	Banishing and releasing negative energies, transformation, enlightenment
SILVER	Wisdom, psychic ability, intelligence, memory	Spiritual development, psychic development, meditation, warding off negativity
GOLD	Inner strength, self-realization, understanding, intuition	Success, health, ambition, finances, good fortune, divination
BROWN	Endurance, solidity, grounding, strength	Balance, concentration, material gain, home, companion animals
GRAY	Stability, contemplation, neutrality, reserve	Complex decisions, binding negative influences, reaching compromise
INDIGO	Emotion, fluidity, insight, expressiveness	Meditation, clarity of purpose, spiritual healing, self-mastery
PINK	Affection, friendship, companionship, spiritual healing	Romance, spiritual awakening, partnerships, children's magic

TOOLS OF FIRE

As we have seen, candles are powerful, versatile, and easy-to-use magical tools that connect us to our ancient past and to the energy of the Universe through the Element of Fire. And while the ways in which candle magic works can be mysterious, they are not altogether incomprehensible. You now have a basic understanding of the role the candle plays in the manifestation of your magical goal. The next step is to learn more about how to choose your candles wisely and get them ready for magical work. Part two provides an overview of the many different types of candles commercially available and instructions for clearing, charging, anointing, and carving them in preparation for spellwork. We'll also explore some divination methods to try with your candles and review practical tips on extinguishing candles, working candle magic with the right timing, and more.

PART TWO

PREPARING FOR CANDLE MAGIC

WICKS AND WAX

THE CANDLES MADE BY THE ANCIENT EGYPTIANS, AND LATER the ancient Romans, were made with reeds or papyrus dipped in rendered animal fat. Thankfully, candles have come a long way since then (though some DIY fans still like to use tallow, which is beef or mutton fat, to make candles the old-fashioned way). Today, making your own candles is considered a hobby rather than a necessary household task.

Not all candles are equally suited for every kind of magical work. Shapes, sizes, colors, burn time, and even wax types can make a difference when it comes to your experience with candle magic. In this section, you'll find descriptions of the most common types of candles available for purchase, their recommended uses, and any required accessories. Then we'll cover how to prepare, or consecrate, your candles for magic. You'll also find some additional advice for making the most out of your spellwork, including setting clear intentions and communing with the energy of Fire after the work has been completed.

CHOOSING YOUR CANDLES

O FTEN, CANDLES ARE PURCHASED FOR A SPECIFIC SPELL, though plenty of Witches keep a stock of candles in commonly required colors. Others might buy tea lights in bulk and reserve a few for spellwork while using the rest for everyday atmosphere enhancement. In fact, using candles for more than just ritual and spellwork is a good habit to develop. If you can, keep one or more candles lit frequently while at home, particularly in the evenings, as these sources of natural light enhance the energetic charge of your environment, whether you're working magic or not.

Candle Shapes and Sizes

These days, countless varieties of candles are available for sale in big box stores, supermarkets, gift shops, and occult or Wiccan supply stores, as well as through online retailers. Some are more suited for single-use spellwork, while others are better for keeping on the altar, marking the circle, or simply lighting the sacred space. Some spells may require a specific type of candle, but many will leave the choice up to you. To that end, here are the main types of candles best suited to ritual and magical work, and some factors to consider when making your choice.

Tea lights are great for their versatility and portability. These small, round candles come in tins or with plastic bases and can be used in a variety of containers, including votive jars, bowls, and lantern holders, or even just on a flat surface—without spilling melted wax. Tea lights are most widely available in white, but you can find them in a variety of other colors. They can get very hot on the bottom, especially those in tin bases. You need to be careful about what you set them on, and you should wait several minutes after extinguishing them before touching the base. If you buy tea lights in bulk, they can be an inexpensive option, and it is nice to always have one on hand.

Votive candles are shaped similarly to tea lights but are generally twice their size. They don't usually come with bases, so they require votive holders, which are often sold near the candles themselves in stores. If you don't want to use a votive holder, you'll need a plate or other flat surface, and you'll need to be okay with the wax melting all over the surface as the candle burns down. Some Witches embrace the "mess," making it part of the magical process and even divining messages from the Spirit world in the shapes of the melted wax, as we will see on page 69.

Votives come in a variety of colors, and there are several Witchcraft and New Age–centered businesses with lines of specially charged votives for enhancing various aspects of daily life, such as prosperity, harmony in the home, or emotional well-being.

Tapers and other long, thin candles require candlesticks and may burn quite messily, depending on the type of wax and the strength of any air currents near the flame. However, a candle of this shape made of clean-melting wax and burned in a still space may leave very little dripped wax behind. It's always wise to avoid placing a new kind of candle on a surface you care about, such as your altar or treasured furniture, until you know how the wax will behave when it melts. If you end up with a holder too big for the base of the candle, you can melt a few drops of wax into it and then hold the bottom of the candle firmly into the wax as it cools and becomes solid again. The cooled wax will support the candle.

Pillar candles, like tapers, are vertically oriented but are much wider. They tend to drip less as they burn, though they still need to be placed on a safe flat surface. Depending on the candle, it may still be best to place a flat dish underneath it. Pillar candles make great "work candles," which are not part of the spell but add extra energetic ambience to the work.

For a guaranteed dripless melt, nothing beats a **jar candle**, which is particularly well suited for repeated use. However, depending on the width of the top of the jar, these can eventually be difficult to relight as the wax level decreases. A long barbecue lighter or long matches are recommended for working with

these candles. One type of jar candle often used in spellwork is the **seven-day candle**, which is pillar-shaped and contained in glass, like the devotional candles used to honor saints. These are great for spells meant to last for a full week—you'll find an example on page 87.

Finally, there are what are usually referred to as **spell candles**, which are sometimes sold as "prayer" or "wish" candles. These small, taper-style candles are generally 4 inches (10 cm) in height and a ½ inch (1 cm) in diameter. These single-use candles are typically inexpensive and come in a variety of colors, each with its own properties and magical associations. Spell candles are sold in many Wiccan and occult-oriented shops and online. You can even buy them in bulk in some places, which is a fun and handy way to save some money. They require quite small holders, which may be a bit more difficult to find than holders for more conventional tapers. But they can burn cleanly if well balanced on a flat dish. (This should only be done when there is zero chance of the candle being disturbed and tipping over.) Witches love spell candles because they can burn all the way out on their own in a relatively short period of time (typically between 1 and 3 hours), making them ideal for spellwork. If you can't obtain these particular candles in your area, don't worry. As always, it's the intention and energy you put into your spellwork that truly makes the magic happen.

Wax Types and Other Considerations

Beyond size and shape, there are other considerations involved in choosing candles for magical use: the type of wax, the average burn time, and whether or not the candle is scented. If you're just getting started using candles, consider trying out a few different types to find the best ones for you.

Most inexpensive candles are made with paraffin wax. Paraffin is a by-product of processing petroleum and thus is not the most environmentally friendly option. It's also been found to release potentially harmful chemicals when burned. However, unless you're extremely sensitive to smoke or burning multiple candles all day, every day throughout your home, it's unlikely that you'll suffer health issues from paraffin wax.

Soy candles are a nice alternative to paraffin candles, as they are sourced from renewable materials. Some also believe they result in better air quality. However, both soy and paraffin can emit soot, particularly if you don't trim the wick before lighting the candle. Soy candles are typically more expensive than paraffin, but they tend to burn longer, so depending on the purpose for the candle and your budget, they can be a worthwhile investment.

Beeswax candles have become more widely available over the past decade, and they can often be found in many of the shapes and sizes described in the previous section. While they are more expensive than paraffin and soy candles, many believe them to add an extra special boost to their magic. This is due both to the lovely honey scent and the natural source of the wax—our friends the bees! While many people may find it too extravagant to use beeswax candles exclusively, they are nice for special magical occasions and may be particularly powerful for spells that work with the Elements of Earth and Air.

The length of burning time is another factor to think about, particularly for candles used in spells that require you to leave them to burn out on their own. If you don't want to be up half the night waiting for a candle to finish, look for those with relatively short burning times, such as tea lights or spell candles. Candles meant to be in use through many rituals should have longer burning times. With the exception of seven-day candles, which can be left burning in a safe place such as a pot of water in a bathtub or sink, *never* leave a burning candle unattended. Even the most conscientious people can accidentally start a terrible fire, so it's always better to be safe than sorry!

The question of scent is also a big one. Some Witches prefer to work with scented candles, but others may prefer to do the scenting themselves by anointing the candle with essential oils. Others find scents distracting and prefer plain wax. If you choose scented candles, look for those made with essential oils rather than synthetic fragrances, which have been found to be toxic to humans and bad for the environment. (Besides, once you've worked with naturally scented candles, you'll likely find that the artificially scented ones really smell horrible!)

As mentioned earlier, some candles on the market have been prededicated or precharged for specific magical purposes. These are often wonderfully scented with natural essential oils and can be used in meditation, as powerful energetic boosters of your magic, or as the central focus of a spell. Some practitioners of the Craft are skeptical of the "store-bought" factor of these candles and prefer to begin with a "blank" or uncharged candle, while others enjoy working with them. They can be particularly handy for beginners, as they can lend an "extra spark" to those just learning to work with their inner power. However, if you work with a predesignated candle, you should still charge it with your own energy before using it for magic.

What about "flameless" candles? The recent proliferation of battery-operated LED candles has some interesting implications when it comes to Witchcraft. These candles lack a literal fire component, but their electrical aspect can still be seen as a representation of the Element of Fire on a symbolic level. Some of the fancier options flicker to emulate the movement of an actual flame and can be turned off by blowing on them. You can even program them to change colors as they "burn," adding an even more magical touch. Flameless candles are also easy to decorate with various materials that might pose a fire risk with actual candles, such as paper or ribbons. They also last far longer than real candles, provided the batteries are replaced (or recharged) as needed.

Many Witches have adopted flameless candles into their practice due to safety concerns or environmental considerations, such as the presence of pets or young children or sensitivity to candle smoke. For those involving children in their magic, flameless candles can be ideal. Children are already excellent pretenders, and a candle they're allowed to hold will be mesmerizing enough that a real flame isn't necessary to get them into a magical mindset! Flameless candles can also be a good choice when it comes to atmospheric lighting and marking the sacred circle for ritual. Some Wiccans may use them for their God and Goddess representations on the altar, depending on the circumstances. However, they generally are not considered ideal for candle-focused spellwork, as the functions of elimination and transformation aren't present. If you can't use candles in your home, try finding a place outdoors where you can work candle spells.

MAGICAL PRACTICALITY

ANDLE SHOPPING CAN BE QUITE FUN, BUT IF YOU'RE NEW TO the Craft and concerned about your budget, don't feel the need to go out and buy every type of candle you can find all at once. There are a few different ways to conserve your funds when it comes to acquiring candles and accessories. Secondhand shops, flea markets, and yard sales often have votive holders, candlesticks, and even candles themselves. If you find a barely used pillar candle for a quarter at a yard sale, feel free to use it for atmospheric lighting, after clearing it first of unwanted energy (see page 48). Just avoid a used candle in your ritual and spellwork.

Some who are new to the Craft may wonder whether a candle purchased from a Wiccan store or occult website is going to be more powerful than one purchased at a grocery or department store. The truth is that if you believe this to be the case, then it very likely will be so. It is nice to get a candle from a source that respects the Old Religion and makes its goods available specifically for the purpose, but not everyone has the luxury of walking into their local Witch shop and stocking up on magical goods. You can order from an online Wiccan retailer, of course, but waiting for shipping isn't always an option. Those on a tight budget may have to use candles from the big-box store or no candles at all. Remember you can always charge your "ordinary" candles to be just as delightfully magical as anything you'd find in a specialty shop.

What if you don't have the right candle (or candles) on hand for a particular spell or magical purpose? Perhaps you're dealing with a breakup and having a hard night of it. You want to do some focused work for emotional healing but find yourself fresh out of pink candles. You don't have to rush out to the store or order a special healing candle online (though you can do this, if you prefer). You can use what you have on hand, including, and especially, your own creativity and intention.

For example, maybe you have a white, unscented tea light and some herbal teas in your kitchen. You can use a white candle in place of any other color candle in spellwork, as white is composed of every color in the visible light spectrum. You can augment the spell with other ingredients corresponding to your goal, to enhance the vibrational frequency of the "missing" color. In this example, you can find some dried chamomile or valerian to sprinkle around the wick of the tea light. Maybe you have some dried wildflower petals or are able to pick a small bunch from somewhere in your neighborhood to enhance the soothing energy further.

For a simple spell in these circumstances, do some freewriting about how you're feeling, which helps to release the energy of your emotions into the Universe. You might tear the paper you've written on into pieces, light them from the candle flame, and let them burn in a fireproof dish. Then set the intention to draw healing energy into your being. Get creative by working with what you have. You can and should create your own spells once you're comfortable doing so.

It can also be useful to let what you have on hand guide the intention and direction of your work. Using your knowledge of the magical properties of the color of the candles you currently have (along with any other ingredients, such as herbs or crystals, you feel called to work with), you can come up with a spell that addresses a problem you didn't even know existed. For example, say you want to do a spell for prosperity but lack most or all of what the spells you're consulting require. Looking around, you find that you have a violet or indigo candle, which is associated with matters of emotional and spiritual insight. Consider the possibility that the Universe is telling you that there are other issues to work on before you are truly ready for the kind of prosperity you seek. This kind of improvisation is easier once you've been learning and practicing for a while, but it can provide opportunities to go down unexpected paths, perhaps discovering that you have a particular need you weren't consciously aware of.

PREPARING YOUR CANDLES

LIKE ANY OTHER TOOL USED IN MAGIC, CANDLES ARE FAR, FAR more effective if they are specifically prepared for use in ritual. It's also important to distinguish between candles you use simply for atmosphere and candles you use for magic. Never work a spell using a candle that has already been lit for another purpose, even if it was only for atmosphere. While altar candles devoted to deities, Elements, and the like may be used repeatedly until they burn all the way down, candles at the center of the spellwork should be new and consecrated for the purpose.

There are many different ways to go about energetically preparing your candle. Terms for the process and the number of steps it involves will depend on the tradition of each practitioner, but the objective is essentially the same. Often called consecrating, this preparation usually includes at least two steps, though many Wiccans add a third step called anointing.

Clearing

Most people will first clear (or "cleanse") their candles of any residual energy. This could be energy left from a prior owner or even someone who gave you the candle as a gift. The energy could also come from the manufacturing process of the candle or the store where it was purchased. Cleansing the old energy, or "psychic debris," from magical tools is done on a deeper level than just physically removing dust or dirt (although that may also be necessary as a preliminary step). What's required here is a *vibrational* clearing away of any energetic imprints that may obstruct the path of the intention as it makes its way into the spiritual realm.

The terms *cleansing* and *clearing* can be used interchangeably to describe the same process, but they present slightly different analogies for how it works. Cleansing is very close to "cleaning," which may bring up images of scrubbing an object vigorously to remove something dirty or foul. To some, this term seems to assume the presence of at least a small amount of negative energy in the object, which may or may not be the case. Clearing suggests a somewhat gentler process, with a more neutral assessment of the energetic remnants to be removed. If you intend to host a gathering in your living room, you'll most likely prepare by getting rid of any clutter that would be in the way or be a distraction for you and your guests. Clearing an object removes energetic clutter in much the same way.

Clearing your candles creates an unobstructed opening for you to channel your personal energy through the candle, and, in the case of spellwork, to charge it specifically for a particular purpose. Clearing is strongly recommended not only for spell candles, but also for candles you use on the altar to honor deities or Elements and even candles that simply serve to light the ritual area. Taking the time to clear all of your candles will enhance the energy of the space and the work being done.

There are many, many methods of clearing items used in magic, but not all are appropriate for every kind of item. For example, athames can be cleansed by passing the blade through a candle flame, but this isn't ideal for a candle itself, as it will melt the wax. Gentler ways to remove old energy include burying the candle in a bowl of salt and leaving it overnight or laying the candle out under moonlight. Both salt and moonlight eradicate unwanted energetic residue, and moonlight has the added benefit of charging the candle as well. If you use salt, it's best to discard the salt afterward, as it will have physically absorbed the unwanted energy and won't be good for further use.

Alternatively, you can light a smudge stick of sage or cedar and run the candle through the smoke to purify it. If you don't have a smudge stick, certain incenses with cleansing properties, such as lavender or sandalwood, can also do the trick. Candles that feel particularly in need of a stronger cleansing can be held under running water (keeping the wick dry) or rubbed gently with a small amount of rubbing alcohol on a soft cloth. With both methods, dry the candle with a clean cloth afterward.

Many Witches consider the clearing to be part of the preparation for a specific ritual or spell. Others like to clear their candles as soon as they acquire them, particularly if they hold any trace of stagnant or otherwise unpleasant energy. As always, do what feels right for you. This may vary depending on the particular candle or the purpose you're using it for. However, it's advisable to refresh any objects that have been sitting around for a long time collecting dust or stored among non-magical itemst before using them. If you're the type to stock up and save, wrapping your candles in tissue paper or cloth after clearing them and storing them with other magical tools is a nice way to keep them ready to use. You'll learn to sense whether a candle or other tool you have had on hand for a while could use some energetic sprucing up.

Charging and Consecrating

The next step, charging the candle, offers a way to communicate to the spiritual plane that you are working to change some aspect of your reality. Many Witches consider charging to be the act of consecration, while others distinguish between consecrating and simply charging an object. There are several methods for completing this process, but all involve charging the candle with magical energy. Not every candle is necessarily going to be used directly in a spell, however, so the way you charge your candles may depend on how you plan to use them. Candles used for atmosphere, for example, are usually cleared and often charged, but are generally not consecrated.

A low-key and low-maintenance method is to lay the candle on a cleansed, charged crystal for a day or two, or at the very least, overnight. As mentioned earlier, moonlight both cleanses and charges, and a Full Moon infuses objects with the strongest charge. Sunlight works as well, as long as it isn't too warm for the candle—you don't want the wax to start melting before the spellwork has even started! These approaches are particularly well suited for atmospheric candles and also work for altar candles representing deities or Elements.

For spell candles, you might want to get a little more involved. Hold the candle in your hands and focus on your goal. Visualize your positive personal power infusing the candle from the base to the wick. Sit quietly for a few moments with your eyes closed, feeling the energy of the candle come alive. If you're charging it well ahead of when you'll use it, place it on your altar until it's ritual time.

Once your candles are cleared and charged, you can take the final step of consecrating them for their purpose. Typically, ritual candles and spell candles are consecrated, but not every Witch consecrates their spell candles. This decision is entirely up to you.

Words are a powerful tool of magic, and most Witches consider them essential to the act of consecration. Chants, prayers, or affirmations spoken aloud (or silently, if need be) help you focus your energy on the task at hand and communicate your specific intentions directly to the unseen world. While Wiccans following particular traditions may have specific words they say every time they perform a consecration, others prefer to create their own blessings. You can use one of the following examples, or come up with your own verbalization of the transformation you're initiating.

Words of consecration typically state a connection among the person, the person's higher power, and the object being consecrated. For example, it's traditional to invoke the God and Goddess, as in this blessing:

"Through the Universal power
of the Goddess and the God,
I consecrate this candle
as an instrument of magic.
Blessed Be."

Witches whose focus is less on deities and more on non-gendered entities of divine power may choose to invoke the Elements, instead:

"Earth, Air, Fire, and Water
come together in me
to charge this candle
with magical power
for the good of all
and harm to none.
So let it be."

When charging a candle for a specific goal, you can include the goal in your words. For example, you might say:

> *"I charge this candle*
> *through the Universal power*
> *to bring good luck and health*
> *to all in my household.*
> *So let it be."*

Whatever words you choose, you should be comfortable with what you're saying. If these examples feel overly formal or inauthentic to you in the moment of saying them, then the consecration is not likely to be successful. Forge your own path in transforming your candles into magical objects by choosing words that have personal meaning for you.

Anointing

Many practitioners add a third step, called *anointing* or *dressing* the candle with magically charged essential oil. For some, this is not a third step, but part of consecrating the candle, to be done while speaking words like those offered earlier. Others may anoint the candle as part of the spellwork itself. Some Witches rarely, if ever, use oil, so this is not an absolute requirement, but if anointing candles is intriguing to you, it's a great way to enhance your spellwork.

If you've charged your candle with magical energy without directing the energy to a specific purpose, anointing with oil is a great way to prepare the candle further for the spellwork you'll be doing. Witches typically anoint just the spell candle itself, but some use oil on every candle involved in Wiccan ritual. As the heat of the candle releases the aromatic properties of the oil, the scent can greatly enhance the ritual atmosphere. Because the candle itself

still holds magical power, oil is not inherently necessary for working magic. Like just about everything in Wicca and Witchcraft, the use of oil is up to the individual's personal preference. That being said, the oil may be the most important ingredient in some particular spells. If the spell you're working insists you use it, it's a good idea to follow those instructions.

Wiccan supply shops sell a variety of magical oils, often as special blends for particular purposes, such as love or abundance spells, or blends tailored to the magical associations between certain oils and zodiac signs, planets, Elements, and specific Sabbats. Some also sell single essential oils, which can be used on their own or combined with others to make your own magical blends. For example, patchouli is associated with prosperity. Patchouli also has a peaceful energy, so if you want a good combination for stress reduction, you can boost your spellwork by adding another oil to it, such as lavender, which is good for working to remove anxiety. On the other hand, if you want to make a prosperity blend, you might add bergamot and cinnamon to the patchouli, as they are associated with success and luck.

No matter where you get your oils from, avoid synthetic fragrance oils, if you can. Synthetic oils are made with potentially harmful chemicals, rather than natural materials, and they don't have inherent magical properties. By contrast, essential oils are derived from plant matter—herbs, flowers, resins, and roots—and have medicinal and magical properties. They have a variety of uses in Wiccan practice, including in ritual baths, as an alternative to incense, as fragrance worn on the body, and of course, for anointing candles. Like candle colors, each type of oil has particular magical properties and associations (see the table on page 56) and can enhance a candle-centered spell.

Always follow instructions for using essential oils carefully, as many oils are not safe to put directly on the skin without a carrier oil to dilute their strength. Carrier oils are vegetable oils like olive, almond, jojoba, and grapeseed oil that dilute the potency of the essential oil but still "carry" its scent. Once you've blended the essential oil with the carrier oil, it's wise to do a patch test to make sure the oil won't irritate your skin. (This is especially true for those with sensitive skin!) Dab a cotton swab in the oil blend and apply it to your inner wrist or behind your knee. Place a waterproof adhesive bandage over the spot and leave in place for 24 hours. (If any irritation occurs, remove the bandage and wash the area with soap and water, and refrain from using the oil again.)

Recipes for homemade magical blends are widely available. If you lack access to essential oils, if they're out of your budget, or if you're simply into a DIY style of magic, you can fashion anointing oils by adding dried herbs to olive or sweet almond oil. They may not have the aromatic component that essential oils have, but they'll still have the magical properties of the herbs. You'll find instructions for making your own herb-based oils on page 115.

COMMON ESSENTIAL OILS AND THEIR MAGICAL USES

ESSENTIAL OIL	GENERAL MAGICAL USES
BERGAMOT*	**Promotes energy, success, and prosperity** *Do not use if skin will be exposed to sunlight. Avoid during pregnancy and breastfeeding.
CINNAMON*	**Increases psychic connections; promotes healing, success, and luck** *If using in anointing oil, do a patch test before applying as it can irritate sensitive skin. Avoid during pregnancy and breastfeeding.
CLOVE*	**Provides protection, bolsters courage, banishes negative energies, cleanses auras** *If using in anointing oil, do a patch test before applying as it can irritate sensitive skin. Avoid during pregnancy and breastfeeding.
EUCALYPTUS*	**Supports healing and purifies** *May irritate skin: do a patch test first.
FRANKINCENSE	**Relieves stress, aids meditation, brings heightened spiritual awareness**

ESSENTIAL OIL	GENERAL MAGICAL USES
JASMINE*	**Strengthens intuition and inspiration, promotes sensuality and love** *Avoid during pregnancy and breastfeeding.
LAVENDER*	**Supports healing, cleanses, removes anxiety** *Avoid during first trimester of pregnancy.
PATCHOULI	**Attracts prosperity, increases lust, boosts physical energy**
SANDALWOOD	**Clears negativity, promotes balanced energy flow**
YLANG-YLANG*	**Promotes happiness, calms anger, enhances sexual attraction** *Avoid during pregnancy and breastfeeding.

To anoint your candle, place one to three drops of oil on the fingertips of your dominant hand (also known as your "power hand"). Use more or less oil according to the size of the candle. A small spell candle, for example, might need only one drop. Holding the candle in your other hand, rub the oil into it, making sure to choose the starting place as well as the direction deliberately, rather than simply spreading the oil all over the candle in a random fashion.

Most traditions hold that there are two ways to anoint the candle, depending on whether your spellwork is for bringing something, such as prosperity, to you or pushing something, such as a bad habit, away. For attracting positive things, you can start at the top of the candle and rub the oil in a downward motion toward the middle. Stop at the middle and then work upward from the bottom of the candle toward the middle. For banishing unwanted things, start in the middle and rub the oil upward to the top, then move from the middle to the bottom of the candle. Alternatively, you can rub the oil from top to bottom for banishing or clearing, and from bottom to top for attracting or creating. You may wish to try all of these different methods to see what feels right to you.

It is extremely important to take precautions when working with oil, especially if you're anointing the candle as part of the spellwork itself. Oil is flammable, so apply a light coating if you're not going to leave it time to dry. Too much oil can cause the flame to burn too high or overpower the wick, and there's risk of burning your fingers, if you're not careful. To be on the safe side, you can use a cloth (consecrated for the purpose, of course) as a buffer between your fingers and the candle and to wipe off any excess oil before handling a match or a lighter. If the oil is skin-safe, you can also dab leftover oil onto your pulse points to strengthen the magical connection between yourself and the candle.

To enhance the magical energy of your candle further, you can roll the oiled candle base in crushed herbs that correspond with your magical goal. For instance, dried rosemary can boost a candle used for a spell that attracts love. You can learn more about magically potent herbs and their common uses in spellwork using the table on pages 60–61.

= COMMON =
MAGICAL HERBS

HERB	GENERAL MAGICAL USES
BASIL	Fosters loving vibrations, protects, wards off negativities in a home
CHAMOMILE	Brings love and healing, relieves stressful situations
CINNAMON*	Brings love, luck, prosperity, and success; raises spiritual vibrations *If using in anointing oil, do a patch test before applying as it can irritate sensitive skin.
HIBISCUS	Supports divination; brings dreams, love, and lust
*MUGWORT	Enhances psychic powers, protects, increases lust and fertility *Do not handle if pregnant or breastfeeding.

HERB	GENERAL MAGICAL USES
ROSEMARY	Enhances love and lust spells, promotes healthy rest
STAR ANISE AND ANISE	Brings luck; boosts spiritual connection, psychic, and magical power *If using in anointing oil, do a patch test before applying, as it can irritate sensitive skin
THYME	Attracts loyalty and affection, enhances psychic abilities
VALERIAN	Protects, drives away negativity, purifies sacred space
YARROW	Supports healing, divination, and love; promotes courage and confidence

Coordinating Your Preparations

Charging and anointing you candle should happen close to the time of the spellwork, if possible. While this is ideal, doing all the preparations right beforehand may not be possible, particularly if you only practice magic within the larger context of a full Wiccan ritual. We live in a busy world, and not everyone has more than an hour to devote to spellwork in a given day. Just as busy cooks might chop vegetables the night before preparing a meal, some Witches may, out of necessity, end up charging and consecrating their candles (or other tools) well ahead of the actual spellwork. This is fine, but keep in mind that the energy used in preparing for ritual is just as much a part of magical work as enacting it. If you don't have much time between the end of your day and the ritual itself, leave yourself a few moments to calm your mind and prepare to focus on magic before handling your precharged candles and spell ingredients.

CARVING SYMBOLS

ETCHING A SYMBOL OR OTHER MESSAGE INTO WAX IS A common element of candle magic. Runic symbols work well for this, as do other, more modern-day representations, such as a peace sign for a spell to resolve an argument or a dollar sign for a money spell. If the work is on behalf of someone else, you might use their initials, and some Wiccans will carve symbols representing the Goddess, the God, some other deity, or one or more of the Elements.

In spellwork, the carving is usually done during the focused ritual itself, but some Witches may do it in advance, using the activity as a way of getting in the right mind frame for magic. To carve a symbol you can use your athame, a reasonably sharp crystal point, or another sharp tool that has been cleared and charged for magical work. (Sewing pins are popular options.) As you carve, visualize your magical goal, making sure to focus on the end result of the spellwork as if it has already manifested. If you're devoting the candle to a deity or Element, visualize the positive power of the divine energy surrounding you and working through you. This will enhance your connection with this energy when you light the candle during ritual.

EXTINGUISHING YOUR CANDLES

MANY CANDLE SPELLS, ESPECIALLY THOSE INVOLVING short-burning spell candles, call for allowing the candle to burn all the way down on its own, rather than extinguishing the flame. If this is the case, be sure that the candle is in a safe place (away from drapes or any other flammable material) before leaving your altar or other magical workspace, and never leave a burning candle unattended. As an extra precaution, you might gently place it in a sink, a large ceramic bowl, or a cauldron large enough to contain the candle as it melts. Just be sure that there is nothing nearby that could catch fire if the candle were to somehow get knocked over! If you typically work spells at night, it's wise to use smaller, shorter candles that won't take several hours to burn all the way down. Again, spell candles are very handy for this reason.

For some people, keeping an eye on a candle as it burns out on its own may simply not be an option, whether due to time constraints, small children who get into everything no matter what, or pets who are likely to get too close to the flame. Worrying about the possibility of injury or fire damage is sure to reduce the effectiveness of the spell, as is worrying about "ruining" the spell by extinguishing the candle. Fortunately, there is an alternative approach to spellwork that calls for a series of lightings over a few days instead of requiring a single, complete burn of a candle.

In this method, the intention set during the first lighting is repeated each night of the spell, strengthening the overall power of the message being sent out into the Universe. Depending on your goal, this may prove a better method than a single-night spell. A few of the spells in part three will make use of this method. Once you've gotten more comfortable with spellwork, you can adjust the spells to your needs by turning a single-night spell into a longer one, or vice versa. The more you personalize your magical work, the more powerful it is likely to be.

Of course, not every candle needs to be left to burn out on its own. While this is often the case in candle magic, other candles used in Wicca, such as ritual deity representations or work candles for atmosphere, are often used several times before they're burned all the way down. For extinguishing these candles, using a candlesnuffer is ideal, though not strictly necessary. Some Witches wave their dominant hand briskly back and forth over the flame until it goes out. This needs to be done carefully, of course, and can be messy if you're working with drippy taper candles.

There is debate among different traditions over whether blowing out a candle is ever permitted. Birthday customs notwithstanding, some Witches consider this to be disrespectful to the Element of Fire, while others believe that doing so as gently as possible is fine if you are sure to thank the Fire respectfully for lending its power to your work. For what it's worth, both waving and blowing tend to produce some great swirling images in the resulting smoke. As with anything else in magic, listen to your inner voice when deciding how to extinguish your candles. Following someone else's instructions when you don't agree with them is not likely to produce successful results.

WITCHY ADVICE FOR
SUCCESSFUL MAGIC

AS YOU'VE NO DOUBT GATHERED BY NOW, MAGIC ISN'T A single event that begins and ends with the working of the spell itself. Your attitude going into the work and your thoughts and actions after the work are important steps for manifesting what you desire. Before moving on to the spellwork in part three, review these suggestions and keep them in mind as you embark on your magical adventures.

Harm to None

First, it's important to acknowledge the effects, and the process, of the time-honored forces of Nature that make magic possible. Like Fire, magic requires care and caution. And when it comes to candle magic, you are *literally* playing with Fire, both on the material and spiritual planes. The old advice to "be careful what you wish for" comes into play here, as any work done with sufficient focused intention is going to have some kind of effect. There can be unforeseen, unwanted consequences—not just for you but for others around you as well.

To use a very extreme example, let's say you're working magic for a new job. A few days later, a cook at a nearby restaurant breaks an ankle and can't come to work for three months, so a job opens up and you get hired to take his place. Now, it's arguable that this cook must have had his own karmic lessons to learn at this time, and that the injury and resulting job loss are part of his soul's plan for personal growth in this lifetime. You certainly didn't intend for anyone to get hurt when you performed your job-finding spell. Nonetheless, there might be a connection here, since the cook could have easily ended up working through his karmic lesson in a way that didn't involve injury or losing a job at this time. Again, this is an extreme example, but it shows how unintended consequences can arise from magical work when we are not careful.

This is why it's important to specify, when stating your intention, that the work be done "for the good of all, and with harm to none." You don't have to use this exact phrase, but the point is to state to the Universe that you do not want any ill effects to occur in the process of manifesting your intention on the material plane. If you always remember to use "harm to none" with your spellwork, you can rest assured that you won't inadvertently cause trouble for others.

After the Work: Reflection and Divination

In candle magic, as in any form of magic, the spellwork takes center stage. However, what happens after you gather your ingredients, speak your intentions, and light the candle is also important. It's highly recommended that you close your magical ritual with as much focus and intention as you had while performing the work. Don't rush off right away to make a phone call or wash the dishes! Not only will you probably feel "out of sorts" from abruptly changing from one energetic state to another, but the magical intention won't get the optimal send-off to have an effect. Instead, spend some time in quiet reflection and commune with your candle. Allow yourself time to transition from the altered state of consciousness induced by magical work back into the mundane quality of everyday life. Acknowledge the changed energy in the space where the spell was worked, and thank the spirit world for its presence.

Experimenting with pyromancy is another way to make the most of your magical work once the spell is completed. As we saw in part one, flames can make for excellent divinatory communication. Spend a few moments contemplating the flame of your spell candle. (To avoid irritating your eyes, keep your gaze trained on the bottom part of the flame, and don't forget to blink once in a while.) As you gaze into the flame, watch for any particular shapes that seem to come up from the wick. Is the flame leaning toward you? Away from you? Notice how it thins as it stretches upward and then widens as it drops back. In some traditions, it's said that if the flame is high and strong, the work is proceeding quickly, while a low, weak flame indicates that not much spiritual energy is being invested in the cause.

It's also said that a wick that produces black or thick smoke indicates there is active opposition to the work. This could be coming from a person, an unknown set of circumstances, or even the unconscious mind of the person working the spell. Remember, however, that different types of candles burn differently, so it helps to get familiar with the way a certain type burns before jumping to any conclusions based on how an individual candle behaves.

As you gain experience, you'll start to appreciate the unique qualities of each and every candle you work with. No two candles burn exactly alike, which you can easily see by burning two seemingly identical candles at the same time. They will drip at different rates, and the flames will move in different ways. Some may crackle and hiss as they burn out while others may be silent.

Don't forget to look for images in the smoke as it twists and curls up toward the sky. You may see hearts, faces, spiraling circles, or other images that have significance for you. With practice, you can learn to get a feel for how the Universe communicates with you through these signs and symbols. If you feel inclined, wave your hand back and forth through the plume of smoke and then observe any images created by your movement.

Another really fun and interesting way to augment your magical work after a spell has been cast is to "read" any melted wax left behind. Known as *ceromancy*, this form of divination doesn't tend to come easily to many beginners, but if you have any practice with scrying in water or a crystal ball, you should be able to adapt these skills to interpret the shapes, forms, and patterns left by melted candle wax. While some candles will burn fairly cleanly so that few or no wax drippings remain, others will melt all over the place, providing opportunities to receive messages from the spirit world regarding the situation you've been working magic 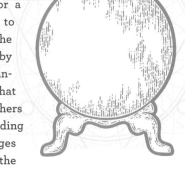 for. Some people will purposefully place votive candles on plates, rather than in candleholders, for this purpose. Many taper-style candles tend to drip profusely, so these can also be good to work with if you're wanting to experiment with ceromancy and don't mind a mess.

As you gaze over the melted wax, look for shapes and patterns that suggest anything about the forces taking shape around your request. In which direction did the air push the wax as it melted? What does the "mood" of the wax's overall appearance seem to be?

Record your impressions in a journal or Book of Shadows, and return to them when more is known about the situation to see whether your interpretation was correct. In this way, you can develop your own symbolic system of ceromancy and grow more adept at this form of divination as you continue to work with candle magic.

Trusting Right Timing

As busy people in a modern culture that often prizes convenience and speed above all else, it can be easy to assume a spell hasn't worked if we don't see immediate results. It's important to recognize that magic has its own process and its own timing, which may or may not align with our wishes. If a spell doesn't seem to be working, there could be many reasons why. It's possible that there just isn't a way at this time to manifest what you want in a way that is for the good of all and harms no one. Sometimes we work spells for things we're not ready for, such as romantic relationships or new homes. Spells can take varying lengths of time to come to fruition, and sometimes, by the time the manifestation occurs, the person who cast the spell has long forgotten it. You can also inadvertently "cancel" the power of your magic because you doubt whether or not the spell worked. If you begin doubting, you are sending the Universe a message saying "never mind about that spell, I didn't mean it."

It's always important to maintain trust in right timing when it comes to magic. However, if you feel certain, after three weeks that your magic didn't work, you may want to try again with more confidence and better focus or a different spell altogether. Don't feel like a failure if your first attempt (or even second and third!) doesn't pan out. In addition to correct intention and timing, magic takes practice.

LET THE FLAMES BEGIN

SO YOU'VE GOT YOUR CANDLES CHARGED AND YOUR MAGICAL goals in mind, and you're ready to try your hand at spellwork. Part three features several spells for help in matters of love, career, money, health, and other important aspects of life. If you're brand new to magic, it's best to follow the spell directions exactly so that you can focus on your intention and avoid wondering whether you really should have skipped a step or omitted an ingredient. And remember that magic takes practice, so if your first spells aren't immediately successful, don't lose faith. Keep experimenting with spells that interest you, and you will eventually see results.

PART THREE:

CANDLE SPELLS AND MAGICAL CRAFTS

A CANDLE MAGIC
GRIMOIRE

THIS COLLECTION OF SPELLS AND OTHER MAGICAL WORKINGS can be considered a short grimoire (an old-fashioned term for what Wiccans call a Book of Shadows). Most of the candles, tools, and ingredients called for in these spells are readily available, if they're not already part of your magical practice. If you don't live near a Wiccan shop, try finding herbs, oils, and even crystals at businesses specializing in alternative healing modalities.

As mentioned in part two, if you have trouble acquiring any of the essential oils, you can make your own herb-based magical oils with ingredients from your kitchen. Instructions and a few suggestions for herbs to use are included in the recipe on page 115. And remember to only use new candles that have been consecrated for the spell's specific purpose. If a spell does not call for the candle to be burned all the way down, you can reuse it for atmospheric lighting, but don't use it for other magic or for representations in ritual.

One fun way to boost your spellwork is to use ideal magical timing. This isn't necessary, but many Witches find that working with the rhythms of linear time makes for more effective magic. Generally speaking, the waxing phase of the Moon is for magic that attracts things into your life, while the waning phase is for releasing old or unwanted things. Likewise, the days of the week have traditional magical purposes:

- ✦ **SUNDAY:** healing, protection, business and career success, spirituality
- ✦ **MONDAY:** home and family matters, peace, healing, psychic awareness
- ✦ **TUESDAY:** passion, competition, protection, strength, lust, courage
- ✦ **WEDNESDAY:** inspiration, study, wisdom, divination, understanding
- ✦ **THURSDAY:** money, prosperity, success, material gain, generosity
- ✦ **FRIDAY:** love, friendship, comfort, arts, beauty, reconciliation
- ✦ **SATURDAY:** long-term projects, wisdom, karmic lessons, endings

It's okay if you can't time your spellwork with these correspondences, but making the effort can help you develop a structure and rhythm for your magical practice.

Remember to take some time to prepare yourself for magic so that you can be fully present, rather than robotically going through the motions, and keep your thoughts focused on your goal. Whether you prefer to cast a circle, meditate, or use other methods for attuning to Universal energies, doing something to distinguish between magic time and the rest of your day will ensure that you're in the right frame of mind to have an impact.

Finally, if you've been practicing for a while and you feel inclined to make a tweak here or add a step there, then go for it! As always, no matter your level of experience, let intuition be your guide.

LOVE AND RELATIONSHIP SPELLS

MATTERS OF THE HEART ARE ONE OF THE MOST COMMON REAsons that people seek out magic. It's understandable to want to do whatever it takes to bring love into one's life. However, beware of spells designed to "win" you the person you desire. Spells that aim to manipulate someone else, no matter how well intentioned, are not considered responsible magic and are very likely to backfire. It's important that you focus on the *situation* you desire, rather than the *person* (or their behavior), when working these spells. After all, you never know what's around the corner—the person you have a crush on today may pale in comparison to someone you're about to meet next week!

MOONLIGHT LOVE ATTRACTION SPELL

For singles who want to enjoy the dating scene, here's a simple spell to heighten your ability to attract potential suitors. This is particularly good for those who have been single for a long time and may struggle to remain optimistic about their prospects.

≡ WHAT YOU WILL NEED ≡

Work candle for atmosphere (optional)

Cinnamon, jasmine, or lavender incense

1 pink spell candle

Crystal point, athame, or other ritual carving tool

**Small vial of wearable essential oil blend
(choose love-promoting scents, such as jasmine,
rose, patchouli, or ylang-ylang)**

≡ INSTRUCTIONS ≡

Light the work candle, if using, then light the incense. Using the crystal point or other carving tool, carve a heart in the center of the spell candle. Place the candle in a window, ideally one with a direct view of the Moon. (If this isn't possible, visualize the Moon as you set the candle down.)

Anoint your wrists, temples, third eye (the center of your forehead, between your eyebrows), and heart with the oil. Then place the vial in front of the candle so that it stands between the candle and the window.

Take a few moments to call up the feelings of well-being, excitement, and companionship. Hold this feeling as you get ready to light the candle. As you light it, say the following (or similar) words:

"By this Moon's light, let my love shine bright."

Allow the candle to burn all the way down. Wear the oil when you go out to help you stay confident in your ability to attract new love.

SPELL FOR FINDING YOUR IDEAL PARTNER

This spell is ideal when you're ready to move beyond casual dating and want assistance in manifesting a solid, healthy relationship. You'll be focusing on what you're truly looking for in a partner, so spend some time preparing for the spell by identifying the qualities you desire. You may want to do some journaling first to help you hone your focus. As an added boost, you can consult color meanings and choose a candle color that aligns with the qualities that are most important to you.

For example, if you know that sharp intelligence and an ability to work well with language are key, you might choose a yellow candle. If you desire someone who is comfortable with expressing their emotions in a healthy way, work with a blue, violet, or indigo candle. If no colors or qualities stand out to you, then go with a white or pink candle.

1 spell candle in a color of your choice

1 gold or silver ribbon, long enough to wrap around your palm at least twice

Pen and piece of white paper

≡ INSTRUCTIONS ≡

Light the spell candle, and wrap the ribbon around your non-writing hand.

On the paper, write down the specific things you desire in a partner for a long-term relationship. Be sure to include how you want to feel around this person and how you want this person to treat you, as all the desirable characteristics in the world won't matter if you're being mistreated in any way. Fold the paper into a small square, then unwrap the ribbon from your hand and tie it around the folded paper. Hold the bundle together in your palms as you meditate on how you will feel in this relationship. Imagine sitting with your new partner, comfortably enjoying the energy of your connection.

Allow the candle to burn all the way down. Place the bundle under your mattress and keep it there for one week, then bury it in a potted plant or in the yard.

SPICE UP YOUR
RELATIONSHIP SPELL

Those of us who are already in long-term relationships may sometimes long wistfully for the rush of feelings that accompanies the beginning of a romance. While you can't turn back the clock to your relationship's early days, you can rejuvenate the atmosphere between you and your partner with this simple spell. This spell can be done during any point in the Moon's cycle. If you're working during the waxing phase, focus on the energy you want to bring into the relationship. During the waning phase, focus on ridding the relationship of any "humdrum" feelings or stagnant-seeming energy.

═ WHAT YOU WILL NEED ═

2 red votive candles

Jasmine essential oil (or homemade love oil blend—see suggestions on page 115)

Plate for melting candles

Pinch of rosemary, fresh or dried

═ INSTRUCTIONS ═

Anoint the candles with the oil and stand them next to each other on the plate. Sprinkle the rosemary on top of the candles and in a circle around them. Light the candles and say the following (or similar) words:

"As these flames dance side by side, so we two renew our stride, in love and in desire."

It's ideal to let the candles burn out in one sitting, but it's also fine to snuff them out and repeat the spell the next night, if necessary. Once they have melted all the way, take some time to look at the melted wax and see if any impressions or messages about your relationship emerge.

SHADOW WORK FOR HEALING RELATIONSHIPS

The term *shadow work* is borrowed from Jungian psychology, but many Witches use it to refer to the aspects of ourselves—our personalities, beliefs, and thought processes—that we are typically unconscious of. Often these aspects are ones we would prefer not to be aware of, such as selfish desires and attitudes, or unconscious fears that can be traced back to traumatic experiences in childhood.

Whenever we have conflict within relationships, whether with friends, family, coworkers, or romantic partners, aspects of our shadows are usually involved. It is our reaction to another's behavior that creates conflict, even when we feel that the behavior is the cause of the problem. When we allow ourselves to become aware of the aspects of our shadow that are at the root of our discomfort, we can get clarity on a conflict and then release the negativity it creates. We can also learn to see conflict as an opportunity to heal and clear the issues within us that are coming to light.

This is a good spell to prepare for with a ritual bath, meditation, or other activity that puts distance between you and your everyday mundane reality. The goal is to approach the situation with neutrality and objectivity, so don't try this when you're actively upset about it.

Choose whichever color feels most resonant with you for the spell candle. The options suggested here are all associated with the Element of Air, which is the domain of new understanding, clarity, and communication.

≡ WHAT YOU WILL NEED ≡

1 black taper or pillar candle
1 blue, indigo, or yellow spell candle
Journal or writing paper and pen (optional)

≡ INSTRUCTIONS ≡

Set the black candle near a wall or other vertical surface so the candle casts a shadow against it. Don't set it so close that it might scorch the wall, and be sure to use a candleholder. Set the spell candle on your altar or another stable surface.

Light the black candle, and with your eyes closed, take three deep breaths. Release all thoughts from your mind, just for an instant. Then open your eyes and just talk out loud for a little while about what you want help understanding about the conflict. Don't complain about the behavior you're upset about. Instead, ask questions that focus on yourself and your response to the situation. For example, you might ask:

"What is it within me that causes this reaction when [name of person] does or says [actions or words that cause hurt]?"

"How can I respond differently and more productively next time?"

*"What is it about myself that I have the
opportunity to learn right now?"*

Now spend some time focusing on the shadows created by the candle and its flame against the wall. Observe the interplay between light (fire) and dark (shadow). As your focus softens, you may see shapes or images that provide insight into *your* shadow—in other words, the underlying cause of what is bothering you about the relationship. Don't worry if you don't get clear visual clues, though. You are still sending your request for understanding into the Universe, and the Universe will respond.

When you feel ready, light the spell candle and spend 10 to 15 minutes freewriting near the light of its flame. Just write whatever comes through your mind, whether or not it seems related to the focus of the spell. When you're finished, gently extinguish the black candle and allow the spell candle to burn out on its own.

You will ultimately receive new insights into the situation, whether through your freewriting, an upcoming dream, or communication from the person you're in conflict with. Just remember to keep your focus on what you are learning about yourself at this time, and let that lead you to a path that heals the relationship.

MONEY AND PROSPERITY SPELLS

MANY SKEPTICS OF MAGIC WILL ASK, "IF IT WORKS SO WELL, why don't people just cast spells to win the lottery?" If only it were this simple. Magic works in cooperation with physical reality, which means the mathematical odds of winning the lottery are still in play. You're also competing with the wishes and dreams of potentially millions of people, and whether they're working spells or not, their intentions factor into the equation. Furthermore, winning money may not be in your best interest in the grand scheme of things—just look at all the tales of woe among those who strike it rich unexpectedly.

Wiccans and other Witches know that we have to do our part in manifesting wealth, by working, making smart choices with money, and focusing on the abundance we already enjoy, no matter how it compares to what we ultimately want. As you develop your magical abilities, be sure to acknowledge and express gratitude for all gifts from the Universe, even for the penny you find on the sidewalk. Let no good luck be considered "too small." Otherwise, the Universe may interpret your attitude as disinterest in experiencing good luck!

QUICK "POCKET CHANGE" MONEY SPELL

This is a great spell for beginners, as it can have immediate and surprising results, even if it doesn't impact your life in a major way. Stay relaxed and open to the possibility of money coming in from unexpected sources, and enjoy the fun of magic!

≡ WHAT YOU WILL NEED ≡

Work candle for atmosphere

Crystal point, athame, or other ritual carving tool

1 green spell candle

Money-focused anointing oil, such as cinnamon, patchouli, or a homemade blend (see suggestions on page 115) (optional)

1 coin, big enough to set the spell candle on

≡ INSTRUCTIONS ≡

Light the work candle. Carve a dollar sign, or the sign of your currency, into the green spell candle. Anoint the candle with the oil, if using. Then hold it in your hands for a few moments and repeat these (or similar) words three times:

"As like attracts like, this money brings more."

Light the candle, set it on the coin, and allow it to burn all the way down. Carry the coin with you in your purse, wallet, or the pocket of some item of clothing that you wear daily for one week.

SEVEN-DAY RENT
AND BILLS STABILITY SPELL

If you often end up scrambling to get the bills paid, or are in a transition period and unsure of how your finances are going to work out in the near future, this is a good spell to help you establish some peace of mind about staying afloat. Once you've sent this spell energy out into the Universe, you can focus on manifesting more long-term improvements to your financial life.

≡ WHAT YOU WILL NEED ≡

Almond oil, or patchouli or bergamot essential oil

Pinch of dried basil

1 seven-day candle, preferably gold, gray, brown, or orange

**1 check from your checkbook (or a piece of paper
that is the size of a bank check) and pen**

≡ INSTRUCTIONS ≡

Anoint the top of the candle with one or two drops of oil. Sprinkle the basil over the oil. Focus on the feeling of ease that comes with having everything in order financially. Light the candle as you say the following (or similar) words:

*"All is provided to me exactly as I need it,
with harm to none. So let it be."*

Sit with the candlelight for a few moments and write some positive affirmations about money and stability on the check or piece of paper. Be sure to write as if the magic has already worked. For example, you might write, "All bills are paid, and I can move forward with confidence." Make sure you use words that resonate with you and help you strengthen your belief in your ability to manifest positive change. Fold the check (or paper) into thirds, then keep folding it until it's as small as you can make it. Place it in your purse or wallet and carry it with you until your bills are paid.

Leave the candle to burn out on its own in a pot of water in a bathtub or sink. This typically takes 7 days, though if positive circumstances are manifesting at a more rapid rate, the candle may burn down more quickly.

BANISHING MONEY BLOCKS

Many people have unconscious attitudes about money that prevent them from ever getting what they desire. We may say we want a bigger salary or more in our savings account, but when we look at our circumstances and can't see any solutions, we conclude that it's impossible. Or we may think that wanting money at all is a sign of greed that goes against our better, "spiritual" natures.

Unlike most money-related spells, this one is best worked during the waning Moon, as it focuses on releasing these unhelpful, and often unconscious, attitudes and fears. If you've been unsuccessful at other spellwork to attract money, you might want to give this one a try. It could be that you've been unknowingly getting in your own way!

Ideally, this spell is worked over 3 to 7 consecutive nights (depending on how many individual blocks you identify), as it's more effective to concentrate on releasing one money block at a time, rather than all in one sitting. This is entirely up to you—follow your intuition when deciding how to pace this work.

═ WHAT YOU WILL NEED ═

1 black taper or spell candle

Journal or other writing paper

1 piece of white paper

Scissors

Cauldron, sink, or other safe place to burn paper

Pen

Light the candle and sit quietly for a few moments. Spend some time journaling about your fears around money. What are the first things that pop into your mind? These are usually the thoughts that block our progress toward prosperity. As you write, see if you can gain any insight about where you picked up these thoughts and beliefs. Are they from your parents? Friends? Society in general?

Now, on the single piece of white paper, name each fear you've identified in a simple sentence. Leave space in between each sentence so that you can cut the paper into strips.

Cut the first "money fears" sentence from the top of the paper. Read it silently and then speak its opposite out loud. For example, if you've written, "I will never have enough," then say, "I always have more than enough." Then light the paper on the candle and allow it to burn out in your cauldron, sink, or other fireproof container. When the strip has finished burning, gently extinguish the candle.

Repeat this spell each night, burning one fear sentence per night, until you've burned them all.

To really seal the work, avoid reusing the candle for any purpose and dispose of the remaining candle stub or bury it in the Earth far from your home.

CIRCLE OF ABUNDANCE SPELL

Feeling prosperous and abundant is essential to *being* prosperous and abundant. If you are constantly focused on what you lack, it can be much harder to manifest it into your life. This spell creates an energetic experience that you can recall any time you want to summon a feeling of abundant well-being. It will help speed up the flow of new abundance into your life.

You will surround yourself, literally, with representations of abundance that are already in your life. Use items that you truly appreciate to get maximum results from this spell. They can be keepsakes, jewelry, artistic creations, photographs of loved ones, and even favorite food items. Some can be things you've had for a long time, while others can be relatively recent acquisitions; don't buy anything just for the spell (unless you need to restock on candles). Make sure each item has a strong, positive link for you with a feeling of abundance and well-being.

Although new abundance will come into your life as a result, this spell is not designed to bring about a specific manifestation. Let your focus remain on the feeling of abundance, rather than on a particular desire for something that you want to bring into your life. The process is about witnessing the flow of abundance generated by your energetic frequency and showing yourself that your *feeling* of abundance is what manifests the flow.

White tea lights work well, but you can use any color or combination of colors that resonates with you.

7–9 tea lights
Several small-to-medium sized items you cherish
Pillow (optional)
1 green, gold, or white pillar candle
Journal or writing paper and pen (optional)

≡ INSTRUCTIONS ≡

Arrange the tea lights in a circle on the floor. The circle should be big enough for you to sit comfortably in the center, so spread the candles at least a foot apart (30 cm). Now fill in the boundary of the circle with the items you've chosen to represent abundance and well-being. You can do this in whatever manner you wish, so more than one item can sit between each pair of candles. Just create an arrangement that is visually and energetically pleasing to you.

When the circle is complete, step inside it and light each of the tea lights, starting with the cardinal direction of North (which represents the Element of Earth) and moving clockwise until the circle is completely lit.

Now sit in the center on the pillow, if using, and place the pillar candle in front of you. Starting with the item you feel the most drawn to in the moment, take time to consider each of the objects forming your circle, one by one. Focus on what you appreciate about each item, including any positive memories or associations it evokes. Think of as many positive aspects as you can. When you feel you've fully appreciated the item, move to the next item, shifting in your seated position as necessary. Notice yourself feeling better and better as you rotate around in the center of the circle.

When you return to your starting point in the circle, take a deep breath and light the pillar candle as you say the following (or similar) words:

> "I am surrounded by abundance.
> I am surrounded by well-being.
> In every place I find myself,
> Let this feeling surround me.
> And so it is."

Now sit and just enjoy the energy you've created for a few more moments. If you like, freewrite about how it feels to appreciate what you have or about anything else that comes to mind. When you're ready, gently extinguish the tea lights and exit the circle, carefully bringing the lit pillar candle with you.

Place the pillar candle on your altar or another surface where you'll see it frequently. Allow it to burn for at least several minutes, if not longer. Whenever you find yourself stressing or focusing on what you don't yet have, relight the pillar candle and call up the feeling of abundant well-being that you created during this spellwork.

WORK AND CAREER SPELLS

COMPARED TO LOVE AND MONEY, WORK MAY NOT BE AS obvious of a focus when it comes to magic, but since most of us spend a hefty portion of our waking hours at work, it makes sense to take a magical approach to improving our circumstances in this realm of life. Job hunting, for example, can be stressful even in the best of times, but working magic for landing a job can make the process exciting rather than dreadful, as it keeps you open to the as-yet-unseen possibilities that your spellwork can bring about. You can also use magic to positively impact the atmosphere at your job and even reduce the unwanted aspects that can make work feel so much like "work."

LUCKY JOB SEARCH SPELL

This very simple spell is great for those who tend to get anxious about whether or not a spell is working, as you have multiple chances to repeat it (though you shouldn't need very many)! Start the spell on a Sunday, which is the day associated with work and career matters, and repeat it, if necessary, each week on the same day.

≡ WHAT YOU WILL NEED ≡

1 gold, green, or orange pillar or taper candle

≡ INSTRUCTIONS ≡

Light the candle as you say the following (or similar) words:

"I am joyfully and gainfully employed,
and filled with gratitude."

Spend a few moments imagining the feelings of relief and excitement that come after being hired for a job you know you will enjoy. Let the candle burn for 9 minutes (or longer, if you wish) as you visualize the feeling of working in a job that you find exciting and well paying. Then snuff the candle out gently. Repeat the spell each Sunday until the candle has burned down completely or until you find a job, whichever comes first.

EMPLOYMENT VICTORY SPELL

So you've applied for a job you want—now what? Boost your confidence and your chances of landing it, with this spell. If you work this spell during a waxing Moon, focus your visualization on beginning the job. If you work it during a waning Moon, focus on winnowing away the competition from other applicants so that you emerge victorious. Be careful here, though, to do it *for the good of all and harm to none*, rather than focusing on causing disappointment for others!

≡ **WHAT YOU WILL NEED** ≡

1 orange spell candle

1 green spell candle

Crystal point, athame, or other ritual carving tool

≡ **INSTRUCTIONS** ≡

On the orange candle, carve a "V" for victory. On the green candle, carve an "F" for fortune. Place them as close together as possible. Light the orange candle, then the green candle. As they burn, repeat this (or a similar) mantra for at least three minutes:

"With this fire divine, the job is mine."

This spell works best if the candles burn out in a single night, but you can repeat it on successive nights until the candle is gone, if necessary.

JOB SATISFACTION SPELL

Most of us find ourselves, at one point or another, having to work at a job we don't like. This may be a part-time job you're doing while attending school, a full-time job you're working because there isn't another option available, or even a position that you planned to be in for the rest of your life. In some cases, the best solution is to find a different way to earn money, even if that means switching careers, moving to a new town, or taking a leap of faith and starting a business. However, when that isn't possible, there's still plenty you can do to improve the way you experience your current form of employment.

This spell helps shift your focus from what you don't like about your work to what's actually going well for you in this context. The more you give your attention to the positive aspects of your current circumstances, the more you will attract circumstances that you enjoy. (Likewise, the more we complain or dwell on the unpleasant aspects of the job, the more we attract things to complain about.) A shift like this usually takes time and practice, which is why using a pillar candle is ideal. With a larger candle, you will have the opportunity every day to reignite the positive energy created by the initial spellwork and to keep track of your progress.

Work candle for atmosphere
Journal or writing paper and pen
1 orange, yellow, green, blue, or violet pillar candle

≡ INSTRUCTIONS ≡

Light the work candle. On a sheet of paper, make a list of things you enjoy (or at least appreciate) about your job. This may include interacting with certain coworkers or regular customers, opportunities to use your unique skills, or aspects of the job you enjoy being good at. Include even what seem like small details, such as a cheerful plant on your desk or a favorite lunch place around the corner.

See how long you can make this list. It doesn't need to be in any kind of order—just write down the details as they come into your mind. Notice how more details pop into your mind as you spend time focusing on these positive aspects of your work. Avoid any thoughts regarding what you don't like about your job, such as coworkers you'd rather do without or tasks you don't enjoy. Don't worry if these details do pop into your mind. Simply let them go and return your attention to the list of positives.

When you're satisfied with your list, fold the paper into thirds. Light the pillar candle and then hold the folded list in your hands as you say the following (or similar) words:

> *"With these words, and with this fire*
> *I manifest more of what I desire.*
> *To be satisfied, to be at peace,*
> *to know I'm working in the right place.*
> *So let it be."*

Now place the folded paper under the candle and allow the candle to burn until you leave the house or go to bed.

Each day before leaving for work, light the pillar candle for at least a few moments, and remind yourself of the items on your list. Then gently extinguish the candle. When you get home from work, light the candle again and spend a few moments appreciating whatever went well for you today, even if it's just a small detail or two. To really maximize the spell, write this down on a new piece of paper (or page in your journal) and keep it on your altar near the pillar candle. (On your days off, leave the candle unlit and enjoy your free time!)

Continue this ritual of positive focus until the pillar candle is completely spent. Take note of how you're feeling about work now—while you're on and off the job—compared to how you felt when you began the spell. If you feel inclined, get a new pillar candle and keep it going!

HEALTH AND HEALING SPELLS

WE KNOW THAT, LIKE ANYTHING ELSE, THE BODY IS MADE of energy. Many popular alternative healing modalities, such as Reiki, qigong, and therapeutic touch, make use of this understanding. Magic, as an energetic process, can also positively affect our health and general well-being.

That said, you should never substitute magic for actual medical care! As with any other "alternative" practice, magic should be used *in addition to*, not instead of, any necessary medical treatment. Just as in money or employment matters, you're expected to do your part to manifest the change you seek, so if you need to seek care or advice from a medical professional, please do so.

SIMPLE HEALING SPELL

For everyday ailments such as the common cold or more chronic issues such as arthritis flare-ups, this spell gently supports the body's natural healing abilities. It can be worked all at once or over a series of days, depending on the nature of the imbalance you're seeking to heal and your preference. If you choose to work it over more than one night, be sure to use a new pinch of yarrow each time.

1 blue spell or votive candle

Pinch of dried yarrow

≡ **INSTRUCTIONS** ≡

Light the candle. Close your eyes and visualize white light filling and surrounding the part of you that needs healing (for example, if you're dealing with a bronchial infection, focus on the lungs). Once you have this image firmly in your mind, visualize the white light growing and expending until it surrounds your entire being. Hold this image for a few moments and notice the shift in your body as you mentally flood it with light. When you're ready, open your eyes and sprinkle a small bit of yarrow into the flame. Thank the Universe for its healing powers and close the ritual with words of confirmation, such as:

"For the good of all and harm to none, this
magical healing work is done."

If you aren't leaving the candle to burn out on its own, wait at least 15 minutes before extinguishing it.

HEALING SPELL FOR LOVED ONES

It can be a wonderful experience to work healing magic for others. However, if you're going to do spellwork for someone else, make sure you get permission first. (If you're not able to be fully open about your magical life, you could just ask the person if they'd be comfortable with you praying for them. After all, magic can be seen as a powerful kind of prayer, and candles are involved in many different spiritual prayer traditions.) In addition, if you're troubled by worries about this person, do some work to release those feelings before working the spell so that you don't inadvertently include the vibration of worry or unease in the intention you're sending to the Universe.

1 white spell candle

Crystal point, athame, or other ritual carving tool

Eucalyptus or lavender essential oil

≡ **INSTRUCTIONS** ≡

Carve the name of the person you're working the spell for into the candle, beginning at the base and working toward the top. Anoint the candle with a few drops of oil, starting at the bottom and working up to the middle, then moving from the top and going back down to the middle. As you prepare the candle, focus your mind on a vision of your friend or loved one glowing radiantly in good health. When you feel ready, light the candle and say the following (or similar) words:

> *"Bright light, this healing white surrounds*
> *and makes [name of person] new."*

Leave the candle to burn all the way down, and continue to keep your focus on manifesting your desire for the person rather than on their current state of health.

BANISHING DEPRESSION SPELL

Those who experience depression often describe it as an unwanted presence in the mind that turns every thought into a sour, mucky experience. It can be very challenging to make use of positive imagery when under the "spell" of depression, so it's helpful to first do some work toward banishing the negative influences underlying this condition. Because the focus here is on banishing, the spell is most powerful during a waning Moon, but don't let that prevent you from using magic to take care of yourself—this process can be worked at any time. As with any spell in this book, this is not a substitute for mental health care. If you are experiencing severe depression or having any thoughts about suicide, please seek help by speaking to a medical profession or by calling a crisis line, such as the National Suicide Prevention Lifeline at (800)-273-8255.

≡ WHAT YOU WILL NEED ≡

3 white tea lights

1 black spell candle

1 small black crystal or stone (such as
obsidian, black tourmaline, or jet)

1 piece quartz crystal (or other white stone)

Small black cloth

Arrange the tea lights in a triangle, and place the black candle in the center.

Hold the black stone between your palms and spend a few moments directing all negative energy from your body and mind into the stone. When you feel ready, place the stone next to the black candle and light it. Say the following (or similar) words:

"I release and banish all negativity from my being."

Next, hold the quartz crystal (or other white stone) between your palms and focus on pulling in healing, loving energy from the Universe. Visualize your entire body flooded with, and surrounded by, white light. When you feel ready, light the tea candles, repeating the following (or a similar) mantra as you light each one:

*"I welcome and trust all positivity and
Universal love into my being."*

Once the black candle has burned all the way down, discard any remaining wax and clean the candleholder before putting it away. Allow the tea lights to burn out on their own.

Use the black cloth to pick up the black stone so that you avoid touching it with your skin, then release the stone back to the Earth as soon as possible. Ideally, toss the stone in a moving body of water, such as a stream, river, or ocean. If this isn't an option, bury it somewhere away from your home. Keep the quartz crystal (or other white stone) in your pocket or in a pouch that you keep near you at all times. You may also want to keep it near your bed while you sleep.

SPELLS FOR OVERCOMING OBSTACLES

HERE ARE A FEW MORE SPELLS FOR TACKLING LIFE'S CHALlenges and making the most of the opportunities that come your way. These spells harness the energy of Fire in its functions of protection, illumination, and attraction.

PSYCHIC ATTACK REVERSAL SPELL

Many resources on magic mention psychic attack, but unless you know other people in your life who practice magic and would want to work magic to hurt you in some way, you're unlikely to become a victim of an overt magical attack. However, because thought is energy, it is possible for the negative thoughts of others to undermine you, particularly if they come from those who may be resentful or envious of you. These thoughts can therefore become a form of psychic attack, even if the perpetrator doesn't intentionally mean harm against us. This spell helps you eliminate any effects that result from the negative thoughts and feelings of others.

5 garlic cloves
1 black candle spell or taper candle
1 teaspoon honey

≡ INSTRUCTIONS ≡

Arrange the garlic cloves around the black candle in the shape of a five-pointed star. Visualize the garlic absorbing any and all negative energy in and around your body. When you're ready, say the following (or similar) words:

> *"I release any and all negativity. I am protected from*
> *all harmful thought from all directions. I am healed*
> *from any harmful effects of the thoughts of others."*

Light the candle, and eat the honey. Allow the candle to burn out on its own. When the spell is done, bury the garlic cloves in the Earth.

HELPFUL ANSWERS SPELL

This spell is for those big, burning questions that just won't leave you alone. While it's often true that we can't know the answer to a question until we're absolutely meant to, you can ask the Universe to send you helpful information in the meantime. The answers may come in a dream, or in a moment of synchronicity in your waking life, such as a phrase spoken in a conversation with a friend or acquaintance.

Just be sure you're open to whatever the answer might be. If you're too attached to a certain outcome, you might not be able to "hear" the truth when the Universe whispers it to you.

═ WHAT YOU WILL NEED ═

1 yellow, blue, violet, indigo, or silver spell candle

1 strip of paper, long enough to
write your question on, and pen

Crystal point, athame, or other ritual carving tool

Cauldron, sink, or other safe place to burn paper

Think clearly about your question and write it as concisely as possible on the strip of paper. Then choose a word that represents the question and carve it into the candle, starting at the bottom and working up to the tip. Light the candle, ignite the strip of paper, and drop it into the cauldron, sink, or other fireproof container. Allow the candle to burn all the way down.

You should receive an answer within 7 days.

CHARM FOR COURAGE

This spell can help you approach any daunting task, whether it's a job interview, a medical procedure, or something more pleasant but still nerve-wracking, like a first date. It's ideal to perform this spell on a Tuesday, the day associated with Mars, which is associated with matters of courage. But don't let this stop you from working this spell on any day you need to.

A charm is any object that has been charged with a specific magical intention. The object can be of any size, but for portable and discreet charms, it's best to use something small enough to fit in your pocket, such as a crystal, a stone, a piece of jewelry, or other small item that has some personal significance to you.

≡ **WHAT YOU WILL NEED** ≡

4 orange spell or votive candles

Clove, cinnamon, or other corresponding anointing oil (optional)

1 crystal, stone, or other small object

Journal or writing paper and pen (optional)

Anoint the candles (if using oil) and arrange them in a square. Place the crystal, stone, or other object in the center of the square.

Spend a few moments identifying a situation from your past in which you felt truly confident and courageous. You may want to brainstorm on paper, letting your subconscious flow until you hit upon a vivid memory. Once you've got a solid sense of this memory, focus on it with all of your attention for a few moments. Pick up the object you've placed in the square of candles, hold it between your palms, and visualize filling it with this powerful courage. You will draw from it later when you need to feel it again.

Place the object back in the center of the square and light the candles, repeating this (or a similar) mantra as you light each one:

"This fire of courage burns always in my heart."

Allow the candles to burn all the way down. Then remove your courage charm from the center of the square. Keep the charm in your pocket (or wear it if it's jewelry) whenever you need an extra boost of confidence.

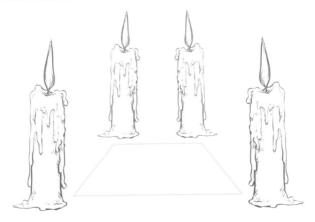

SPELL FOR
CULTIVATING GOOD LUCK

Nearly everyone has experienced a "bad luck streak," when things just seem to go constantly wrong. Few of us realize, however, that we end up contributing to the streak by focusing on the negative and therefore maintaining low-frequency thoughts. It doesn't help that our mainstream culture seems to focus more on what's going wrong (or what could go wrong!) than on all the well-being that exists in our world. We almost reflexively view a string of good luck as rare, or possibly even suspicious.

This spell boosts your ability to attract good luck by counteracting negative thought patterns around luck and fortune. As always, the spell words offered here can be rephrased to suit your individual style. You can use spell candles or candles in a larger size, depending on whether you'd like to repeat the spell.

═ WHAT YOU WILL NEED ═

1 black candle

1 white candle

1 green candle

Pinch of chamomile and/or star anise

═ INSTRUCTIONS ═

Arrange the candles side by side, a few inches apart. Place the black candle on the left, the green on the right, and the white in the center. Sprinkle the herbs and spices in a circle around the candles in a sunwise (clockwise) motion.

Light the black candle and say:

"All bad luck away."

Take a deep breath and visualize your energy field being cleared of any negativity.

Then light the green candle and say:

"All good luck to stay."

Take another deep breath and summon the feeling of knowing that all is well. Sit with this feeling for a few moments, with your eyes closed.

When you feel ready, as you open your eyes and say:

"Open my eyes and my ears to good fortune."

Then light the white candle. Focus on sending your intention to be more aware of *everything* that goes right in your life, no matter how seemingly trivial.

You can allow the candles to burn all the way down, or, if you want to repeat the spell, gently extinguish them.

It's great to work this spell once a week for four weeks, and take notes during this time about what you observe. Record all the positive things that happen to you, but do *not* record any negative things. This spell is about retraining the brain to focus more consistently on the positive, so don't muddy the work with details that don't support your vision of a lucky and charmed life. When you repeat the spell, have your notes with you and spend a few moments in gratitude for the good luck that you have recently noticed.

THE WITCH'S CRAFT

WITCHCRAFT IS MORE POPULAR TODAY THAN IN ANY POINT in history. The explosion of interest over the past two decades has given rise to many Witch-centered businesses offering countless magical products, from spell ingredients like candles, oils, and herbs to fully assembled, precharged spell kits.

Although many of these store-bought items are of high quality and work quite well, you don't have to buy everything you need for successful magic. You can make many magical tools and ingredients all on your own. The DIY approach is not only often less expensive, but it also allows you to infuse your magical creations with your own personal energy and intention right from the start. There are hundreds, if not thousands, of ideas and instructions out there for making various magical crafts. The following pages contain a few candle-related craft ideas to get you started.

DIY MAGICAL OILS

For some people, essential oils can seem like an obstacle to spell-work because they can be cost-prohibitive or difficult to find. The good news is that herbs contain the same magical properties as their essential oil counterparts and have been used in the creation of anointing oils in many magical traditions. You can make your own herb-infused oils with common kitchen and healing herbs that work just as well as any store-bought essential oil blend, even if not all of the homemade oils are aromatic. All you need is a base oil and a handful or two of your favorite magical herbs.

═ WHAT YOU WILL NEED ═

Roughly ½ cup (20 g) fresh or dried herbs*
Base oil, such as olive, almond, or safflower oil
Small mason jar (or other jar with a tight-fitting lid)
Cheesecloth (optional)

*Here are a few suggestions for herbs to use for magically charged oils. You can make single-herb oils or combine two or more. Blends of three herbs are considered to be particularly potent.

- ✦ **PROSPERITY:** basil, bay leaf, cinnamon, nutmeg, patchouli
- ✦ **HEALING:** clove, eucalyptus, goldenseal, lavender, rosemary, thyme
- ✦ **LOVE:** cardamom, cinnamon, hibiscus, patchouli, rosemary
- ✦ **ALL-PURPOSE MAGIC BOOSTER:** anise seed, basil, rosemary, cinnamon

Before you begin, remember to charge your herbs, focusing your intention on the purpose of the oil, whether it's for love, money, or just strengthening magical power in general.

Place the herbs in the jar, then pour the oil over them, covering them by at least an inch (3 cm).

Close the jar tightly, and leave it in a cool, dark place for at least three days. You can then strain the oil through a cheesecloth into another jar. This step isn't strictly necessary, though it will help keep the oil from going rancid for a longer period of time, especially if you're using fresh herbs. (Shelf-life varies from a couple of weeks to a few months, depending on the specific oil and herbs. If it begins to smell "off" or the jar starts to feel sticky, that's a good indication that it's time to make a new batch!)

Use your oil to anoint your candles. You can even apply it to your skin as preparation for working magic, but do a patch test (see page 55) first to make sure it won't affect your skin, especially if the oil contains cinnamon, which can irritate sensitive skin.

DIY Candles and Candleholders

It's hard to imagine now, but candles were not widely available for purchase until the nineteenth century. This meant that most people, including Witches, made their own candles. If you want to get truly back-to-basics crafty, there are plenty of instructions for candlemaking online. Unlike making herbal oils, it isn't necessarily cost-effective, as you'll need to purchase more supplies, but for the craft-obsessed Witch, candlemaking is a fun way to create powerful tools for your spellwork.

You'll need a double boiler dedicated just to this purpose (melting wax will ruin cookware), along with the wax, wicks, and candle molds or other containers for shaping and storing candles (glass jars are perfect). If you're a fan of beeswax, you can purchase beeswax sheets to roll into candles. This works particularly well for candles with thinner shapes, such as spell candles.

If making candles is a little too labor-intensive, you can still take a DIY approach to your candle magic by transforming ordinary objects into magical tools. Seven-day novena candles, for example, which can often be found in grocery stores, can be turned into deity or Element candles for the altar. You can paint these or other jar candles with designated colors and symbols, or cut out and paste images that represent the God, the Goddess, or the Elements you wish to represent with the candle.

If you're finding it a challenge to acquire all the necessary candleholders for the various types of candles you want to use, make your own by decorating small plates, cups, or even shot glasses with magical symbols. And for a unique ritual tool for charging your candles, paint the drainage tray from a small clay pot with a pentacle or another magical symbol. Magic is about creativity, so use your own whenever and however you can!

CONCLUSION

THE INTENTION OF THIS GUIDE HAS BEEN TO PROVIDE A SOLID starting point for your personal practice of candle magic. Now that you understand the basic principles of magic, the properties of colors, and the energy of the Fire, you can begin trying your hand at spellwork with confidence. Follow the spells in part three, but also experiment and create your own spells as you learn to deepen your intuition and psychic awareness. Remember that learning occurs as you go, and it takes time to achieve proficiency in magic, as it does with any other skill. To that end, you'll find suggested resources for further reading on page 123.

No matter how much knowledge you acquire, it's the practice of magic that leads to success. Be willing to try and try again, and you will ultimately develop the ability to transform your life. Remember to keep your intentions clear and positive as you harness the cocreative powers of the Universe. May the energy of Fire be with you!

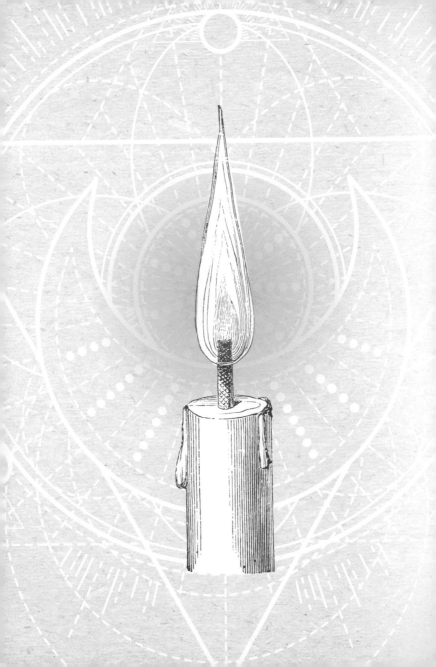

ACKNOWLEDGMENTS

AS ALWAYS, MY DEEP APPRECIATION EXTENDS TO MY BIRTH family and chosen family for their infinite love and support. To Lesley, my first Witchy friend, for her enthusiastic love of fire. To Kate and Elaine, for lessons in the many uses of jam jars. And to Zack, for being an early and essential spark.

To Barbara Berger at Sterling, for her creative vision, and to Elysia Liang for her thoughtful edits. To Elizabeth Lindy for the beautiful cover design; creative director Jo Obarowski; Christine Heun and Sharon Jacobs for the stunning interior design conception, direction, and layout; production editor Ellina Litmanovich; and production manager Ellen Day-Hudson.

SUGGESTIONS FOR FURTHER READING

Below are some further resources covering a variety of methods for working magic with candles. You may find that some of the information in these books differs from what is detailed in this guide. This is due to the wide variety of magical traditions and practices. These differences are also a part of what makes magic so enjoyable and give you the ability to blend your own intuition with time-tested knowledge. As with anything else in Witchcraft, take what makes sense to you and disregard what doesn't. Happy reading!

Buckland, Raymond. *Advanced Candle Magick: More Spells and Rituals for Every Purpose.* St. Paul, MN: Llewellyn, 1996.

———. *Practical Candleburning Rituals: Spells & Rituals for Every Purpose.* St. Paul, MN: Llewellyn, 1982.

Conway, D. J. *A Little Book of Candle Magic.* New York: Crossing Press, 2000.

Cooper, Philip. *Candle Magic: A Coveted Collection of Spells, Rituals, and Magical Paradigms.* Newburyport, MA: Weiser, 2000.

Grant, Ember. *Magical Candle Crafting: Create Your Own Candles for Spells & Rituals.* Woodbury, MN: Llewellyn, 2011.

Lady Passion. *Candle Magic: Working with Wax, Wick, and Flame.* New York: Sterling Publishing, 2017.

Starza, Lucya. *Candle Magic: A Witch's Guide to Spells and Rituals.* Alresford, UK: Moon Books, 2016.

Webster, Richard. *Candle Magic for Beginners: The Simplest Magic You Can Do.* Woodbury, MN: Llewellyn, 2004.

PICTURE CREDITS

INDEX

ABOUT THE AUTHOR

LISA CHAMBERLAIN is the successful author of more than twenty books on Wicca and magic, including *Wicca Candle Magic*, *Wicca Crystal Magic*, *Wicca Herbal Magic*, *Wicca Book of Spells*, *Wicca for Beginners*, *Runes for Beginners*, and *Magic and the Law of Attraction*. As an intuitive empath, she has been exploring Wicca, magic, and other esoteric traditions since her teenage years. Her spiritual journey has included a traditional solitary Wiccan practice as well as more eclectic studies across a wide range of belief systems. Lisa's focus is on positive magic that promotes self-empowerment for the good of the whole.

You can find out more about her and her work at her website, wiccaliving.com